The Lord is Risen!

LUKE 24

EMMAUS BIBLE RESOURCES

Missionary Journeys, Missionary Church – Acts 13 – 20

Steven Croft

Also available:

Travelling Well

Stephen Cottrell and Steven Croft

EMMAUS BIBLE RESOURCES

The Lord is Risen!

LUKE 24

STEVEN CROFT

EMMAUS: THE WAY OF FAITH

The National Society
Leading Education
with a Christian Purpose
Church House Publishing

National Society/Church House Publishing
Church House
Great Smith Street
London SW1P 3NZ

ISBN 0 7151 4971 7

Published 2001 by National Society Enterprises Ltd

Tel: 020 7898 1557
Fax: 020 7898 1449
Email: copyright@c-of-e.org.uk

Cover design by Church House Publishing

Typeset in Franklin Gothic and Sabon

Printed in England by The Cromwell Press Ltd,
Trowbridge, Wiltshire

Contents

How to use this book

The *Emmaus Bible Resources* can be used on your own, with
a small group and with a whole church or group of churches
(or any combination of the three).

On your own

Each chapter is divided into six parts ending with a short prayer
or meditation.

You can use the studies as part of a daily time of Bible reading
and prayer.

Or you can read the chapter with the biblical text at a single
sitting.

A simple Order for Daily Prayer is provided at the back of the book.

With a small group

The group can be three friends, a husband and wife, an ongoing
home group or one drawn together for these studies.

Each member of the group should read a chapter of this book and
the biblical text between meetings.

At the end of each chapter, you will find a 'Guideline for groups'.

Each group will need a convenor to guide you through this material.

With the whole church

The material is designed so that a church or group of churches
could use it as the basis of Sunday and midweek material for
learning and discussion.

A group of Sundays can be identified as appropriate for a series of sermons on Luke 24. Tables of readings and other resources are provided in the Liturgical Resources section at the end of the book.

This book is particularly appropriate for use in the Easter season but it can, of course, be used at any time of year.

Members of the congregation who wish to engage with the text for themselves can then be encouraged to read this book as a study guide alongside the sermon series. Those who wish to do so can also meet in small groups during the week.

Introduction to *Emmaus Bible Resources*

The two disciples walk along the road to Emmaus with Jesus, although they do not recognize him. As they walk together, Jesus interprets and opens the Scriptures to them. They have no books or texts with them but these disciples would already be familiar with many of the words of Scripture and would perhaps have learned them by heart.

From the earliest times, Christians have read the Scriptures on their own, together and in the company of the risen Christ. Every act of Christian worship has at its centre the public reading of the Bible, the word of God. Through reading and study of the Scriptures, our Christian faith is refreshed, strengthened, challenged and renewed. As Paul writes to Timothy:

> All scripture is inspired by God and is useful for
> teaching, for reproof, for correction, and for training
> in righteousness, so that everyone who belongs to
> God may be proficient, equipped for every good work
> (2 Timothy 3.16-17).

It is becoming harder to live as a Christian. Every Christian needs to live out the truth of their baptism: each one of us is called to Christian discipleship and Christian service according to the gifts God has given to us.

The *Emmaus Bible Resources* are offered as a way of encouraging individuals, small groups and congregations to engage with the text of Scripture in order that they may be built up and grow in Christian life, faith and service.

As with *Emmaus: The Way of Faith*, we have tried to combine sound and orthodox Christian theology with good educational practice on the one hand and a commitment to equip the whole Church for mission on the other.

Each book in the series is complete in itself and is intended as a guide either to a passage of Scripture or to a short series of passages grouped around a central theme. We hope to publish two or three books in the series each year. Normally the passage will be part of a longer book within the Bible, or it may be the whole of one of the shorter books.

Each book in the series is largely written by one person (whose name appears on the cover) but has been edited by the original group of authors. We hope, over time, to involve others outside the original group in developing new material for the series.

Each author has been asked to write for a general Christian audience but to bring to the work insights from the Christian tradition of interpretation and the best of contemporary biblical scholarship. Notes and references have been kept to a minimum although there are some ideas for further reading. Each book also encourages a variety of learning styles in terms of individual study and reflection and group interaction.

Wherever possible, some of the material in each book has been piloted both with individuals and in small groups. We are very grateful to the churches, groups and individuals who have assisted in this way. The new series can be used just as well by individuals and churches who have not used the original *Emmaus* material as by those who have been using it for many years.

Five years after the publication of *Emmaus: The Way of Faith*, we are surprised and humbled at the many ways God has used the material, through the ministry and prayers of many Christian people and for the building up of Christians, of churches and, ultimately we pray, of the kingdom of God. Our prayer for this new series is that it may be used by God in similar ways and to the same ends.

Stephen Cottrell
Steven Croft
John Finney
Felicity Lawson
Robert Warren

Acknowledgements

I would like to record my thanks to the Council of St John's College, Durham, for a period of study leave from January to March 2001 which enabled the writing of this book and *Missionary Journeys, Missionary Church*. Particular thanks are due to my colleagues in Cranmer Hall who kindly undertook additional duties for that period.

The publisher gratefully acknowledges permission to reproduce copyright material in this book. Every effort has been made to trace and contact copyright holders. If there are any inadvertent omissions, we apologize to those concerned and undertake to include suitable acknowledgements in all future editions.

Unless otherwise indicated, the prayers and reflections at the end of each section of text are by the author.

Bible quotations are from *The New Revised Standard Version of the Bible* copyright © 1989 by the Division of Christian Education of the National Council of the Churches in the USA. All rights reserved.

Extracts from *Common Worship: Services and Prayers for the Church of England* (Church House Publishing, 2000) and *The Alternative Service Book 1980* are copyright © The Archbishops' Council of the Church of England.

The extract from 'Hallelujah My Father' by Tim Cullen is copyright © 1975 Celebration/Kingsway's Thankyou Music, PO Box 75, Eastbourne, East Sussex, BN23 6NW, UK. Europe & British Commonwealth (excl. Canada, Australasia & Africa). Used by permission (p. 16).

The extract from 'Lord Jesus Christ' by Patrick Appleford is copyright © 1960 Josef Weinberger Limited. Reproduced by permission of the copyright holders (p. 65).

The illustration 'My Wife and Mother-in-law' by W.E. Hill is reproduced with permission of Mary Evans Picture Library (p. 23).

An Introduction to Luke 24

A special time

According to Luke, the 50 days from Easter to Pentecost are a unique period in the history of the Christian faith. Jesus is risen from the dead. The disciples come to believe this great truth over a period of time through a variety of encounters. The risen Christ meets with his followers over 40 days 'speaking about the kingdom of God' (Acts 1.3). After this, he is taken from their sight but commands them to wait in the city, until they are clothed with power from on high. There is a short period of waiting and then, on Pentecost, the fiftieth day, the Holy Spirit empowers the infant Church for mission to the whole earth.

A special book

Luke's purpose in writing his Gospel is not simply to tell us what happened but to enable us to share in the events of Jesus' birth, ministry, death and resurrection. When we hear Jesus' teaching in the parables, we are meant to apply his words to our own lives. When we read of the great miracles, we are meant to wonder with the disciples about the meaning of this for our own day. When Jesus calls people to follow him, we hear the invitation ourselves and respond or turn away. The second half of the Gospel takes us on a great journey from Galilee to Jerusalem and asks us to enter into, especially, the story of the last days of Jesus' life: the entry into the city; the events in the upper room; his trial and crucifixion. As we make this journey with Jesus, our understanding, our faith and our Christian discipleship are strengthened, challenged, deepened and renewed.

In exactly the same way, Luke asks us to accompany the first disciples as they experience the wonderful, world-changing reality of resurrection. Like them, we cannot take it in all at once. With them, we are sometimes perplexed, amazed, doubting and uncertain. We need to come with the women to the tomb in the early morning and see the stone rolled away, the tomb empty, the linen clothes left behind. We need to walk the Emmaus road with Cleopas and the unnamed disciple, in dialogue with one another and with the risen Christ, seen yet not understood. We need to hear again both the call to witness to Christ throughout the world and our need to be empowered by the Spirit for that witness.

A special season

For much of its life, the Christian Church has celebrated the resurrection not simply by setting aside a single day in the year but by setting aside a season: 50 days, from Easter Day to Pentecost, following the pattern given to us by the third Gospel and Acts. These are days for Christians to celebrate, but keeping Easter is about far more than services and meals together, eggs and holidays (although it can be all of those things). The season of Easter is also about taking time to appreciate again the life-transforming gospel of the death and resurrection of Christ. It is a time when we return to the foundation and the centre of our faith, to be renewed and empowered in our own life and witness to that gospel. We become a community being changed from those whose faith and understanding are clouded and uncertain to a Church renewed in its life and witness by the truth of the resurrection and the gift of the Spirit.

Introducing Luke

The book of Acts and the Gospel of Luke are the work of the same author. He is a skilled weaver of individual stories and of the shape of his narrative. The Gospel of Luke tells the story of Jesus beginning with the birth of the Baptist until the ascension of the risen Christ. The Acts of the Apostles begins with the Ascension and Pentecost and traces the mission of the Early Church from Jerusalem and Judaea to 'the ends of the earth' in Rome. The last chapter of the Gospel and the first of the Acts serve to dovetail the two books together and join the two separate stories into one larger whole.

In crafting his Gospel, Luke makes full use of earlier accounts of Jesus' life, ministry and resurrection, especially of the earlier Gospel of Mark. He refers in his introduction to 'many' who 'have undertaken to set down an orderly account of the events that have been fulfilled among us'. These earlier accounts, Luke believes, 'were handed onto us by those who from the beginning were eyewitnesses and servants of the word'. We know from comparing the Gospels that, in addition to Mark, Luke either had access to the Gospel of Matthew or the two shared common source material. The Gospel of John was the last to be written and makes use of and reflects on the traditions passed on by the first three writers.

Each of the Gospels tells the story of Jesus from a different perspective, from within a different faith community, and highlights different concerns through the selection and arrangement of material. We should see them as portraits of Jesus, not photographs, attempting to bring out not simply a likeness or a series of events but depth, meaning and character. Luke is writing for a largely non-Jewish culture. His readers need to have Jewish terms and customs explained to them. The person he pictures in the dedication to the Gospel and Acts, Theophilus, should be seen as a convert to the Christian faith, needing to learn the story of Jesus and of the Church into which he has been baptized.

Neither book was written to be read primarily by individuals at home. Only a small proportion of people could read for themselves and only a very small number would have a copy of a gospel. The books were written on separate scrolls (for reasons of length) and read aloud when Christians met together, either in homes or in larger public assemblies. From earliest times, the public reading of the gospel would be accompanied by teaching, exposition and dialogue on the theme of the reading.

Four accounts of the resurrection

All four of the Gospel writers tell the story of the resurrection of Jesus in a different way. All four begin with the visit to the empty tomb in the early morning of Easter Day by women. These are recognizably four different accounts of the same event, with some details included, omitted or changed. Then, Matthew, Luke and John tell us of different meetings with Jesus in Galilee or Jerusalem. Mark's Gospel ends with the women running from the tomb 'for they were afraid'. Scholars have long debated whether this is how Mark planned to end the story or whether part of the manuscript is lost, since the original Greek appears to break off in the middle of a sentence. Other resurrection accounts have been added to Mark's Gospel in different manuscripts. For the most part, these seem to be abbreviated forms of the encounters in Matthew, Luke or John.

Luke has therefore selected the encounters with the risen Christ in his Gospel from a much larger number and he has shaped them into the story that we find in the last chapter of the Gospel and the first chapter of Acts. In particular, Luke has chosen encounters that fit into a particular framework of time and place. All of the encounters in Luke 24 take place on the first Easter Day (in the early morning, middle of the day and the evening). All of the encounters take place in Jerusalem. Luke chooses not to tell us of any meetings with the risen Christ in Galilee, wanting to keep the focus on the place where the Spirit will fall and the Church will begin.

The shape of this book

The approach taken here is to encourage the reader to see the story of the resurrection and Ascension of Jesus and the gift of the Spirit through the words of a single gospel writer, Luke, as he unfolds and shapes the story under the inspiration of the same Holy Spirit. There is a great deal to be learned about the resurrection of Christ, the message of the gospel, understanding the Scriptures, the way that gospel is to be shared with others and our own need for the power of the Spirit.

The study starts in **Chapter 1** with the story of the early morning and the new day that begins with Christ's resurrection as the women come to the tomb.

Chapters 2, 3 and **4** all focus on the story of meeting Jesus on the Emmaus road which takes up the majority of Luke 24 (vv. 13-35). In the central chapter of the book, we look at some of the passages that may have formed part of Jesus' exposition of Scripture on the Emmaus road.

Chapter 5 is a reflection on Jesus in the midst of the disciples, the great commission that is entrusted to them and the promise of the power of the Spirit. The whole of Luke 24 is bound together by common themes and words: if you don't know it well, it would be helpful to read the chapter through at one go before you begin the first study.

This book can, of course, be read at any time of the year but is designed to be used as an 'Easter book' for individuals, groups and churches (much as you might read a Lent book or study guide from Ash Wednesday to Holy Week). Easter is the period of the year when the Church reflects on the meaning of the resurrection. In churches where the nurturing of new disciples is linked with the cycle of the year, Easter is also set aside for the deepening of the faith and call of those who have been newly baptized. Parts of the Early Church and of the Church today refer to this as the time of 'mystagogy', which means 'contemplating the mysteries' of Christian faith, especially in the sacraments. The book will therefore be especially useful for individuals or groups who have recently been baptized or confirmed or who have taken part in courses like Emmaus, Alpha or the adult catechumenate. Its themes could be linked with post-Easter retreats, walks or quiet days for individuals or groups, as well as to Sunday worship and small group meetings.

The raw material for my own reflections has been working with the Emmaus road story closely over a period of eight years, in company with the other authors of

Emmaus: The Way of Faith. I have had the opportunity to preach and lead Bible studies on this passage in many different settings. I have been both surprised and thankful that a story in Scripture I have loved since I was a child, far from becoming stale for me, has continued to yield new insights into the Christian life. A period of study leave has given me the opportunity for closer study of the surrounding chapter and to set the walk to Emmaus in its wider context of the way Luke tells us that the Lord has risen. I am very grateful to Felicity Lawson and the parish of St Peter's, Gildersome, for testing the material and giving me suggestions on how to improve it.

May God grant you grace to meet with the risen Christ in Christian fellowship, in Scripture and in the breaking of the bread.

Steven Croft
Easter, 2001

Chapter 1
The First Day – Luke 24.1-12

A new dawn

> But on the first day of the week, at early dawn, they
> came to the tomb, taking the spices that they had
> prepared (Luke 24.1).

In the dim light of the early spring morning the small group of women move
quietly through the sleeping city to the burial ground a short distance away.
They carry fragrant spices and ointments, prepared the day before. They come
in fear and grief to wash and anoint the body of one they love and have lost.
Two days ago, on the eve of the Sabbath, the soiled and broken body of Jesus
was hastily wrapped in linen cloth and placed in a borrowed tomb.

The women are from Galilee, many miles to the north. They have left home
and family to travel with Jesus and cared for him in life as they now seek to
care for him in death (Luke 8.1-3). Already their lives have been changed. They
have listened to his stories and heard crowds call both 'Hosanna' and 'Crucify!'.
They have seen healings and miracles, bread broken and wine poured out. They
watched from a distance as he was tortured and killed. They have listened and
looked but do not understand.

Like grieving people everywhere, they draw some little comfort from one another
and from simple, practical tasks. The mind cannot absorb the horror of sudden
death. The pain of grief must be experienced a little at a time. Has it really
happened? What does it mean? We cannot think beyond today.

As Luke's readers, we watch the story of the resurrection unfold through Luke's
words. We come with the women to the tomb. But we have also read the book to
the end. We know what is over the page. Like those who first listened to Luke's
Gospel, we have worshipped in the great congregation on Easter Day. With Christ,
we have passed through the waters of baptism, from death to life. We have joined
our voices in the great Easter acclamation:

> Christ is risen!
> He is risen indeed! Alleluia!

As Luke writes the words 'on the first day of the week' he deliberately echoes the language of creation in Genesis 1. He is announcing the greatest of new beginnings. Jesus has died, yet this is the day of resurrection and new life. This is the beginning of the age of hope and of salvation for all the nations: the fulfilment of all that the prophets foretold, because Christ is risen from the dead. Luke takes the whole of the chapter, one of the longest in the Gospel, to describe for Christian people in every generation the story of this first and perfect day of resurrection.

Yet the story is not one of instant rejoicing. Strong words are used throughout the chapter to describe the emotions and reactions of the disciples: they are perplexed (v. 4), terrified (v. 5), amazed (v. 12), startled (v. 37), frightened (v. 38) and disbelieving (v. 41). We are meant to stand in their place. We would have been the same if we had been present on the first Easter Day. In the way he tells the story, Luke makes it clear to us that the wonder of the resurrection is not something we can embrace in a moment. Joy, like grief or pain, cannot be absorbed all at once. We need to receive and understand it a little at a time until the message affects the whole of our lives.

It's partly for that reason that the Christian Church has developed a pattern of taking the 50 days from Easter to Pentecost to celebrate, to reflect on and to absorb again year by year the wonderful truth of the resurrection of Jesus. We celebrate the feast of Easter for ten days longer than the fast of Lent. Receiving, holding onto and understanding the great truth that Christ is risen is the theme for the whole of that time.

Into this period of reflection, year by year, we come, like the women at the tomb, bringing our own sorrows and burdens. Like them, we have heard and seen but we are only beginning to understand. We need to take time, as we explore this first, perfect day of resurrection, to receive all that it means.

Lord of all life and power,
who through the mighty resurrection of your Son
overcame the old order of sin and death
to make all things new in him:
grant that we, being dead to sin
and alive to you in Jesus Christ,
may reign with him in glory;
to whom with you and the Holy Spirit
be praise and honour, glory and might,
now and in all eternity. Amen.

Common Worship: Collect for Easter Day

Seeing Jesus

> They found the stone rolled away from the tomb,
> but when they went in, they did not find the body
> (Luke 24.2).

Read the chapter as a whole and look at the gradual way in which the disciples meet the risen Christ. The women come to where they expect to see Jesus, but do not find him. They are given clear signs of what has happened: the stone is rolled away, the tomb is empty, two men in dazzling clothes give news of the resurrection. Peter also runs to the tomb, stoops and looks in and sees the linen clothes by themselves. Later we are told the Lord appeared to Simon earlier in the day (v. 34) but Luke does not describe that encounter for us.

The first time we encounter the risen Christ in Luke's Gospel is on the road to Emmaus. Jesus draws alongside, joins in a conversation and is seen yet unseen by the disciples: 'While they were talking and discussing, Jesus himself came near and went with them, but their eyes were kept from recognizing him' (vv. 15-16). Later in the day, in the very moment when they see him, he is gone: 'Then their eyes were opened, and they recognized him; and he vanished from their sight' (v. 31). It is not until verse 36 that Jesus is visible and present with the disciples: 'While they were talking about this, Jesus himself stood among them and said to them, "Peace be with you."' Finally, at the end of the chapter there is fellowship, dialogue, a meal shared and blessing.

What does Luke mean by this careful structure within the unfolding story? He is saying something, certainly, about the grace of the risen Christ: Jesus will not, as it were, force himself upon those who are unwilling to receive him. This is a recurring theme in the chapter, to which we will return. Yet something is also being said about the way in which disciples come to know that Christ is risen, the way sorrow at the beginning is turned to joy at the end.

As Luke represents it, the process of understanding and believing is neither sudden nor simple for the disciples. A number of different elements play their part. The *physical evidence* of the empty tomb is certainly important, but not enough. As we have seen it is clearly established not only here but later in the chapter (vv. 23-24). As Jesus comes to stand among his disciples, physical evidence is again emphasized. He invites them to touch him and to give him something to eat: 'Touch me and see; for a ghost does not have flesh and bones as you see that I have' (v. 39).

The chain of *witness* of other people plays its part all through the story. The two men in dazzling clothes tell the women. The women tell the apostles. Peter tells Cleopas what he has seen. The walkers to Emmaus return and are told by the eleven and their companions and in turn recount their own story. In his commission, Jesus says to them all: 'You are witnesses of these things' (v. 48).

Yet physical evidence and the witness of others alone are insufficient. The testimony of *Scripture* and the remembered words of Jesus are vital in comprehending what has happened:

> Remember how he told you, while he was still in Galilee, that the Son of Man must be handed over to sinners, and be crucified, and on the third day rise again (vv. 6-7).

> 'Oh, how foolish you are, and how slow of heart to believe all that the prophets have declared! Was it not necessary that the Messiah should suffer these things and then enter into his glory?' Then beginning with Moses and all the prophets, he interpreted to them the things about himself in all the scriptures (vv. 25-27).

> 'These are my words that I spoke to you while I was still with you – that everything written about me in the law of Moses, the prophets, and the psalms must be fulfilled.' Then he opened their minds to understand the scriptures, and he said to them, 'Thus it is written, that the Messiah is to suffer and to rise from the dead on the third day, and that repentance and forgiveness of sins is to be proclaimed in his name to all nations, beginning from Jerusalem' (vv. 44-47).

In and through the physical evidence, the witness of others, a new understanding of Scripture, there is also a powerful and personal *encounter* with the risen Christ. This takes place in the exposition of the word of God ('Were not our hearts burning within us . . . while he was opening the scriptures to us?', v. 32). It takes place in the breaking of bread: 'Then their eyes were opened, and they recognized him' (v. 31). It takes place in the greeting of peace: 'Jesus himself stood among them and said to them, "Peace be with you"' (v. 36).

No other generation has had the same physical evidence as this small group of 120 disciples. Yet we do have the benefit of their story. We also have the witness of others through thousands of years that Jesus is risen. We have the evidence of Scriptures that his life, ministry and death fulfil what is written there. We have the opportunity of powerful and personal encounter with the risen Christ in the exposition of the word of God, in the breaking of bread, in the greeting of peace within the Christian community and in our daily walk with God. In the same many and various ways today, through faith, disciples come to understand and to believe that he is risen.

Lord God, creator of sight and hearing,
of understanding and of faith:
open our eyes that we may see your works;
open our ears that we may hear your word;
open our minds that we may understand your ways;
    and
open our hearts that we may trust your Son,
our risen Saviour, Jesus Christ.
Amen.

Perplexed

While they were perplexed about this . . . (Luke 24.4).

The women have come to the tomb with a clear expectation in their minds: Jesus has died. They witnessed his death themselves (23.49). The manner of his death was terrible. The sentence was carried out by Roman soldiers who knew their task well. The women expect to find a body that has been in the grave two days.

Like people of a certain age the world over, the women are only too familiar with death, which robs us of those we love and which never gives them back. They are familiar with the psalms of the Old Testament that cry out to God in anguish and protest that our lives and the lives of others should be cut off, as it seems, and all end in death.

But as they reach the tomb, these deep expectations are confounded. The stone has been rolled away. They do not find the body. They would see, as Peter saw, that the linen clothes are by themselves. What has happened?

This group of women, together with the other disciples, are about to go through a complete change in their view of the world, of life and death, of Jesus and of themselves. What they are about to experience does not fit their present view of how the world works: those who have been crucified do not rise from the dead. The departed cannot return. The empty tomb is the first sign that their view of how the world works is no longer adequate and itself needs to be transformed. Perplexity is the first point in this enormous inner shift. Not understanding something opens the women's minds to new and enormous possibilities.

For us today, the experience is a familiar one. The simple act of walking consists of throwing ourselves off balance and rebalancing with every step. Babies and young children make new discoveries rapidly which gradually change their view of the world. One of the real joys of watching babies grow is the moment they discover their feet. We learn new things by being thrown off balance: new experiences or evidence comes at us which does not fit our existing view of the world or of people or of ourselves. We are perplexed. Gradually, we come to terms with the new evidence and our inner map of how the world works is redrawn little by little.

In scientific discovery, perplexity has often been the key to progress. It is the little things that do not quite fit the accepted theories of the day that are the key to moving forwards. Humankind moved reluctantly away from the idea that the earth is flat, because the evidence began no longer to fit the concept of reality, and just a few began to be perplexed and challenge existing theories. For hundreds of years, people believed that the earth was at the centre of the universe and everything revolved around it. In the sixteenth century, because of conflicting evidence, that view of reality was challenged and our map of the universe was redrawn. The same kind of change is happening every time a person begins to consider the resurrection of Jesus Christ.

In his own teaching, Jesus uses this method of throwing people off balance in order to open them up to a new picture of reality. In the parable of the good Samaritan, the fact that it is the unexpected person, the despised Samaritan, who performs the act of kindness overturns people's stereotypes and prejudice and opens them up to seeing a whole community (and themselves) in a different way (Luke 10.25-37). In the story of the shepherd who leaves 99 to go in search of a single lost sheep, our picture of God begins to be challenged: God is not like a human shepherd. In what other ways might he be different (15.3-7)? In his comments on the widow's offering, Jesus throws his listeners off balance by his declaration that 'this poor widow has put in more than all of them' (21.1-4).

The empty tomb and linen clothes throw the women off balance and open them to new possibilities. They are not, by themselves, the message of the resurrection or even evidence for the resurrection. We could not possibly work out for ourselves what has happened – only that something is different and unexpected. These things are signposts and stumbling blocks to make us think: a preparation for the message of good news that follows.

And that is why all the Gospels take the trouble to mention the empty tomb: to make us think and go on thinking. What has happened to Jesus' body? Was it stolen? Why were the grave clothes left behind? Why was it not produced by the Romans or the Jews at a later date?

For people today there is another searching question of this kind: how do we account for the massive change produced in the disciples over these 50 days? How were they transformed from this small, frightened group of men and women to the core of a community which was known for its joy and courage in proclaiming the gospel in every part of the known world?

Here is evidence that simply does not fit the view that many around us may have: that Jesus died and the early Christians somehow made up the resurrection. The last thing the disciples were expecting was for Jesus to rise from the dead.

Perplexity is often difficult but can sometimes be a friend. It is only as we allow ourselves to be perplexed that our ears will be open for a new understanding of reality: the message of good news.

> Loving Lord, risen from death,
> grant us the courage and humility to admit
> that there are many things we do not understand;
> break down our prejudice;
> grant us a spirit of openness and wonder
> at your work in creation
> and through our perplexity
> help us to hear the good news of your love
> for the sake of your kingdom.
> Amen.

Remember how he told you . . .

While they were perplexed about this, suddenly two men in dazzling clothes stood beside them. The women were terrified and bowed their faces to the ground, but the men said to them, 'Why do you look for the living among the dead? He is not here, but has risen. Remember how he told you, while he was still in Galilee, that the Son of Man must be handed over to sinners, and be crucified, and on the third day rise again' (Luke 24.4-8).

For the first time in Luke, before we encounter the risen Christ, we hear the good news of the resurrection in the words of the heavenly messengers: 'Why do you look for the living among the dead? He is not here, but has risen.'

Heavenly messengers appear at the beginning, middle and end of Luke's Gospel, each time bringing a revelation from God. An angel begins the story, bringing the news of John the Baptist's birth to Zechariah (1.11). Gabriel is sent to Mary in Nazareth, announcing that she will conceive (1.26-31). Angels bring the good news of Jesus' birth to the shepherds (2.9). On the mountain of the Transfiguration, two men, Moses and Elijah, appear 'in glory' talking to Jesus 'speaking of his departure [*exodus*] which he was about to accomplish in Jerusalem'. By referring in 24.4 to 'two men in dazzling clothes' Luke echoes both the story of Jesus' birth and the Transfiguration.

The fact that the resurrection is revealed by heavenly messengers is a sign that it is a message of great importance, directly, as it were, from God himself. Luke stresses heavily both in the Gospel and in Acts that the message of the good news is not something that has been worked out or put together by men and women but is revealed by God from heaven.

The heavenly messengers point the women back to Jesus' own understanding of his destiny, death and resurrection, given to them in Galilee, the place they first came to know him. The shadow of the cross falls over the whole of Luke's Gospel from the words of Simeon to Mary when Jesus is presented in the temple: 'and a sword will pierce your own soul too' (2.35). In Luke's account of Jesus preaching in Nazareth, he is rejected and almost killed (4.28-30).

However, from the moment at which Simon Peter declares that Jesus is the Messiah, Jesus begins to teach consistently about his own death and resurrection. The Jews are expecting a messiah who will fulfil everything written in the law and the prophets (as they interpret the prophecies). This messiah will be a political king who will re-establish Israel through military power and bring freedom from Roman rule. Jesus' own understanding of his ministry is very different. Drawing on different Old Testament traditions, he sees the fulfilment of his life and ministry in his suffering, death and resurrection:

> He sternly ordered and commanded them not to tell anyone, saying, 'The Son of Man must undergo great suffering, and be rejected by the elders, chief priests, and scribes, and be killed, and on the third day be raised' (9.21-22).

Later in the same chapter, after Jesus has returned from the mountain of the Transfiguration, again he foretells his death:

> 'Let these words sink into your ears: The Son of Man is going to be betrayed into human hands.' But they did not understand this saying: its meaning was concealed from them, so that they could not perceive it. And they were afraid to ask him about this saying (9.44-45).

Finally, in chapter 18, towards the end of the great journey to Jerusalem which begins at 9.51, Jesus speaks for a third time about his death and resurrection:

> Then he took the twelve aside and said to them, 'See, we are going up to Jerusalem, and everything that is written about the Son of Man by the prophets will be accomplished. For he will be handed over to the Gentiles; and he will be mocked and insulted and spat upon. After they have flogged him, they will kill him, and on the third day he will rise again.' But they understood nothing about all these things; in fact, what he said was hidden from them, and they did not grasp what was said (18.31-34).

By setting these sayings at the beginning and end of the journey to Jerusalem, Luke implies this was a continual theme of Jesus' teaching. Yet on two occasions he adds the explanation that the meaning of the sayings was hidden from the disciples and they did not grasp what was said. The motif of something being said but not understood occurs elsewhere in the Gospel (8.9-10) and is not unlike Jesus being present with the disciples on the Emmaus road but not recognized by them.

The words of the messengers are addressed to the readers of the Gospel as well as to the women at the tomb. Comprehending the truth of Jesus' resurrection means looking back at the whole of the Gospel and seeing that his death and resurrection were foretold and fulfil his understanding of his own ministry.

> Hallelujah, my Father,
> For giving us your Son;
> Sending Him into the world
> To be given up for men,
> Knowing we would bruise Him
> And smite Him from the earth.
> Hallelujah, my Father,
> In His death is my birth;
> Hallelujah, my Father,
> In His life is my life.[1]

Tim Cullen

© 1975 Celebration/Kingsway's Thankyou Music

An idle tale?

 Then they remembered his words, and returning from the tomb, they told all this to the eleven and to all the rest. Now it was Mary Magdalene, Joanna, Mary the mother of James, and the other women with them who told this to the apostles. But these words seemed to them an idle tale, and they did not believe them (Luke 24.8-11).

Women are the first to learn of the resurrection of Christ, the first to reflect on the words of Jesus, the first to believe the message and the first to pass it on to others. All through the third Gospel and in Acts, Luke gives prominence to the ministry and role of women. These women, in particular, have been with Jesus from Galilee and have shared in the common life of the early community:

> Soon afterwards he went on through cities and
> villages, proclaiming and bringing the good news
> of the kingdom of God. The twelve were with him,
> as well as some women who had been cured of evil
> spirits and infirmities: Mary, called Magdalene, from
> whom seven demons had gone out, and Joanna, the
> wife of Herod's steward Chuza, and Susanna, and
> many others, who provided for them out of their
> resources (8.1-3).

After the revelation at the tomb, these women now return 'to the eleven and to all the rest'. This is the first mention of an assembly that is to be the focal point of Luke's story through the final chapter of the Gospel and into the first twelve chapters of Acts. Throughout the Gospel, the eye of the narrative has followed Jesus closely, until his death. From this point on, the centre of the story is the community of disciples 'numbering about 120' who are left behind. All of the action moves out from and comes back to this group, the earliest Christian church, until the point at which Acts begins to focus entirely on the ministry of Paul (from chapter 13 onwards).

The beginning of the story of the Church is not very promising, however. The gospel is announced to the eleven and the rest 'but these words seemed to them an idle tale, and they did not believe them' (24.11). The word translated 'idle tale' occurs only here in the New Testament and carries the meaning of foolishness, mere chatter. As Luke tells the story, of course, the egg is on the face of the men here for not believing those they have come to know and not remembering the words of Jesus himself. One of the most remarkable features of all of the Gospels is the way in which they recount honestly the faults and failings of the apostles who were the leaders in the Christian communities in which the stories were given shape. It would surely have been a temptation to downplay the mistakes of those who were to have such an extensive ministry.

The eleven still wear the blinkers of the old world view and refuse even to be perplexed. The women can now see what they cannot. They are confronted with the evidence: the empty tomb, which they investigate; the testimony of their companions; the remembered words of Jesus; yet they cannot even begin to take seriously the possibility of resurrection. How well we defend ourselves against profound changes of belief and action! Our grief, our fear of standing out from the crowd, our pride and our prejudice against the opinions of others prevent us from even beginning to see what has become very clear to those around us. How is Christ to overcome our blindness and enable us to see?

The first attempt to witness to the resurrection seems to be a failure. However, the women were not the last Christian messengers to announce the good news of the resurrection and to have their testimony dismissed as foolishness. Within a matter of a few weeks, these same disciples will be giving public witness to the resurrection in their preaching and teaching and meeting a similar response. One of the reactions to Paul's witness to the resurrection in Athens is open mockery (Acts 17.32). On other occasions the same message provokes direct hostility and persecution.

There are many women and men today who bear witness to the truth of resurrection to those closest to them, in their families and among their close friends, and find their witness dismissed as an idle tale and not believed. But a person's first response to a message is not always the last. Because our message is initially mocked or rejected does not mean it is in vain. Although the disciples dismiss the women's words here, the companions on the road to Emmaus continue to ponder what they said. Their testimony forms a link in a chain of understanding which leads eventually to faith.

Prayer suggestion

Pray especially for those close to you who know of your belief in the resurrection but consider it an idle tale. Pray that you may be given wisdom to witness clearly and well to your own faith. Pray that the risen Christ may draw near to your family and friends as they reflect on what you have said.

Peter

> But Peter got up and ran to the tomb; stooping and
> looking in, he saw the linen cloths by themselves; then
> he went home, amazed at what had happened (Luke
> 24.12).

> 'The Lord has risen indeed, and he has
> appeared to Simon!' (Luke 24.34).

Peter is an important figure in Luke–Acts, especially in these chapters of
transition and overlap between the two books. When Peter first appears in
the Gospel, Jesus is a guest in his home after preaching in the synagogue at
Capernaum (4.38). Luke describes Jesus' call of Simon, as he is then known,
following the miraculous catch of fish (5.1-11). Simon is the first named of the
disciples when the twelve are chosen, the only one whose new name is mentioned
by Luke. Peter means 'rock'. Peter is the spokesman for the twelve in declaring
that Christ is the Messiah (9.20). At the Last Supper, he is adamant that he will
not abandon Jesus, yet Jesus tells Peter in advance of his time of testing:

> 'Simon, Simon, listen! Satan has demanded to sift all
> of you like wheat, but I have prayed for you that your
> own faith may not fail; and you, when once you have
> turned back, strengthen your brothers.' And he said to
> him, 'Lord, I am ready to go with you to prison and
> to death!' Jesus said, 'I tell you, Peter, the cock will not
> crow this day, until you have denied three times that
> you know me' (22.31-34).

The use of the nickname 'rock' here surely carries some irony. The last time
we encountered Peter, he was weeping bitterly outside the courtyard of the high
priest, having denied Jesus three times (22.62). The next time we see him in the
story it will be as the recognized leader of the young church in Jerusalem, taking
the initiative in appointing Judas' replacement (Acts 1.15) and preaching the great
sermon to the assembled Jews on the day of Pentecost (Acts 2.14). It is then Peter
who is the most prominent among the apostles until the great council in Acts 15,
when he fades from view to give place to Paul.

In chapter 24, Luke does not portray Peter as the spokesman of the eleven and the rest. We might suppose he lacks the confidence to assume leadership of the group. He neither believes the women nor dismisses what is said but he goes to see for himself. Thus it is that, according to Luke, Peter is granted the first of the resurrection appearances on the first Easter Day, an impression echoed by Paul (who calls Peter 'Cephas', the Greek translation of Peter or rock):

> For I handed on to you as of first importance what
> I in turn had received: that Christ died for our sins
> in accordance with the scriptures, and that he was
> buried, and that he was raised on the third day in
> accordance with the scriptures, and that he appeared
> to Cephas, then to the twelve. Then he appeared to
> more than five hundred brothers and sisters at one
> time, most of whom are still alive, though some have
> died. Then he appeared to James, then to all the
> apostles. Last of all, as to someone untimely born,
> he appeared also to me (1 Corinthians 15.3-8).

The Gospels nowhere describe this personal appearance to Peter. The closest we have to it is the account in John's Gospel of Jesus and Peter walking on the beach after breakfast and Jesus offering Peter the opportunity of a threefold affirmation of his love, with the threefold commission to 'Feed my lambs', 'Tend my sheep', 'Feed my sheep' (John 21.15-17).

However, what is implied in the Gospel story in Luke is very significant. Peter has sufficient faith and hope to run to the tomb and look in. His encounter with the risen Christ, however, is about more than becoming a witness to the resurrection (although it is that). Simon's encounter with the risen Jesus is about forgiveness, transformation and healing: a setting right of what has been wrong. It is an act of grace on Jesus' part. The disciple to whom Jesus appeared first is the one who most needs his forgiveness. In terms of the Gospel story, it is a meeting hidden from our view.

Most of us do not find it too difficult to see ourselves in Simon. We are all too ready to take the lead in the company of other disciples, yet all too easily deny Christ in difficult circumstances through our words, our actions or our lifestyle. The gracious way the risen Jesus deals with a failed disciple should encourage us. In hidden ways and secret places the same Lord is able to meet with us, forgive us, restore us and enable us to move on to the ministry to which he calls us.

Risen Lord,
who saw in Simon the potential to be Peter,
in your risen power,
heal and restore your servants;
help us to hear your voice
and to become the people
you call us to be,
for your glory's sake.
Amen.

Guidelines for groups (1)

This section at the end of each chapter gives guidelines for a 90-minute meeting of a small Bible study group of up to a dozen people. You could also use the material as a guide for a much smaller group of two or three friends or family members (in which case the timings may be different). The guidelines assume that the group members have looked at the Bible passage before the meeting and, ideally, have read through at least some of the reflections in this chapter.

The guidelines are in three parts.

> First, some ideas to help the group members share together some of their own life experiences which will help them gain a new understanding not only of one another but also of the biblical material.

> Secondly, some questions for discussion that aim either to take you further in understanding the Bible or to help you reflect on its lessons for life today. In a larger group, you may need to break down into smaller huddles of three or four people for some of the sections.

> Finally, there are suggestions at the end of each study for an extended time of prayer and reflection together. One of the aims for using the period from Easter Day to Pentecost is to allow time and space for exploring the mystery of our faith not only in discussion but through prayer. If you are reading this book on your own rather than with a group, you may still find some of the prayer exercises helpful, either in your own devotional life or as part of a retreat or quiet day.

Approximate timings are given at the start of each section. However small your group, you would be wise to appoint someone as a facilitator to guide you through the discussion. Feel free to pick and choose the most helpful questions and to develop your own material. No group will be able to do everything in the time available.

Give some thought in advance to where you might meet, the arrangement of the room and food and drink. It will also be helpful to designate one or two different people each week to lead the prayer time.

Sharing together (30 mins)

1. If this is a new group meeting, on the first occasion each person should take a moment to introduce themselves.

2. Each member of the group should say something about their hopes for your meetings together to discuss Luke 24. Ask everyone to give their initial impressions from reading Luke 24.1-12 and the study material. If you can, share one thing you gained and one question you bring.

3. Describe the way in which you celebrated Easter when you were a child and today. What means the most to you? What would you like to change?

4. Look together at this well-known picture. Do you see an old woman or a young woman? Help one another to see the two different pictures in the frame. Does this shed light on the way different people come to 'see' the resurrection of Jesus?

'My Wife and Mother-in-law' by W.E. Hill supplied by Mary Evans Picture Library

Studing together (40 mins)

1. How do you think you came to understand the resurrection of Jesus? What part was played by evidence, the witness of others, the Scriptures and encountering Christ?

2. Look briefly at the way each of the Gospel writers tells the story of the empty tomb and the resurrection. How do you account for the differences and similarities? Why do you think Luke tells the story in this way?

3. 'These words seemed to them an idle tale.' Do any members of the group have an experience of bearing witness to the resurrection and others not believing them? How should we respond in that situation?

4. What do you think must have happened when the Lord appeared to Simon?

Prayer together

1. First, set the scene to allow the group to change gear. You may want to have a two-minute break, rearrange the chairs, or set up a visual focus for prayer such as an icon or candles.

2. Begin with a prayer asking the risen Lord to be present with you. Follow this with a time of quiet: either use silence or a quiet piece of music to allow hearts and minds to be still.

3. The leader should read the Scripture passage slowly, leaving plenty of space between the sections of the passage. Invite the group to imagine the scene as it unfolds. One or two comments and suggestions may be helpful in this process.

4. After you have pictured the scene in your mind, imagine an encounter between you and the risen Jesus at the scene of the empty tomb. What do you say to Jesus? What does Jesus say to you?

5. End with silence, music or a quiet song, and a final prayer.

6. There may be things members of the group want to note down in a journal or share with others. Go on reflecting on the passage, on your meditation and on encountering the risen Christ through the coming week.

Chapter 2
Beginning the Journey – Luke 24.13-24

Setting out

> Now on that same day two of them were going
> to a village called Emmaus, about seven miles from
> Jerusalem, and talking with each other about all
> these things that had happened (Luke 24.13).

The story of the Emmaus road is unique to the Gospel of Luke and is carefully constructed and beautifully told. As a story, it has natural symmetry. There is an outward journey and a return. The story begins and ends in Jerusalem. It begins in sadness and separation but ends in joy and reunion. The eyes of the disciples are kept from seeing Jesus and then opened. There is a retelling of the story of Jesus in outline, and of the visit of the women to the empty tomb. The whole of the gospel is contained within a single episode. Later generations of Christians have seen a balance between word and sacrament. There is rich irony, and even humour, as the two disciples tell Jesus the story of his own life and ministry. The story echoes the account of the feeding miracles and the Last Supper, and is itself echoed in the encounter between Philip and the Ethiopian eunuch on the road to Gaza (Acts 8.26-40).

Jesus himself appears in the story as comforting stranger and familiar friend, as one instructed and as the teacher, as a guest and yet host. The disciples are transformed from downcast doubters and sceptics to joyful witnesses of the resurrection, rushing back to Jerusalem to break the news, only to discover that Jesus has been before them and has appeared to Simon.

The story continues the central theme of perception begun in the first part of the chapter: how did the disciples come to know and understand that Jesus is risen from the dead? Again we see that the process of coming to understand and believe is not the work of a single moment. Nor does it involve simply the mind, or simply the eyes, or simply the emotions. Understanding and believing involves the whole person responding to Christ made known in ordinary encounters, in the witness of others, in Scripture and in the breaking of the bread.

Luke emphasizes at the beginning of the story that it happens 'on the same day' as the visit to the empty tomb. We have here a continuation of his account of the first day of resurrection. Given that the journey is about seven miles, and the disciples arrive at their destination when it is 'almost evening' (v. 29), we should imagine that Cleopas and his companion set out for Emmaus in the late afternoon, after the heat of the day has passed.

By telling the story in the context of a journey, Luke makes a deliberate link both forwards and backwards. This is the way he has structured the second half of the Gospel. From Luke 9.58, all of Jesus' teaching and encounters with individuals are set in the context of a journey to Jerusalem. The story of the road to Emmaus therefore recalls us to the familiar picture of Jesus walking with his disciples, instructing them through dialogue as they travel together. In turn, the journey of Jesus and the disciples recalls the Exodus, the journey of the Israelites out of slavery to freedom in the promised land.

The picture also looks forwards to Acts, much of which will also be structured around the theme of journeys. One of the earliest names for Christianity itself is 'the Way' or journey (Acts 9.2; 19.23; 24.22). We should not, therefore, be surprised if Luke 24 not only tells us about one of the resurrection appearances but also has lessons to teach us about our own journey of faith.

The story is about two unknown disciples. One is given a name, Cleopas, but the other is not. John's Gospel mentions a 'Mary the wife of Clopas' as one of the witnesses of Jesus' death (19.25). Other ancient sources refer to Cleopas as the father of Simeon, who later became a leader of the church in Jerusalem.[1] If that is the case, we might assume that Cleopas himself remained a part of the Christian community in the city and was, perhaps, known to some of Luke's original readers. The tradition has also understood the unnamed disciple on the Emmaus road as a woman, the wife of Cleopas. This is certainly possible, although we would have to assume that this particular woman was not part of the group that went to the empty tomb in the early morning. However, there may be a reason for Luke not naming the second disciple in that he intends us to be able to imagine ourselves into the story, sharing in all that happens along the way and becoming, in time, witnesses of the resurrection.

Almighty Father,
you have given your only Son to die for our sins
and to rise again for our justification:
grant us so to put away the leaven of malice and
    wickedness
that we may always serve you
in pureness of living and truth;
through the merits of your Son Jesus Christ our Lord,
who is alive and reigns with you,
in the unity of the Holy Spirit,
one God, now and for ever.

Common Worship: Collect for the Second Sunday of Easter

The wrong direction?

... going to a village called Emmaus ... (Luke 24.13).

Why are the two disciples leaving Jerusalem? Perhaps they are part of a
general movement of pilgrims away from the city following the Passover.
Some have suggested that they had to find lodgings some distance away from
the overcrowded city and so this would be a daily two-way journey over the
period of the festival.

However, there are other signs that Luke means us to think that the two disciples
are moving in the *wrong* direction as they set out to Emmaus. They are drifting
away from the main group in Jerusalem. Luke sets the city and the gathering of
the believers there at the centre of the story through the end of the Gospel and
the beginning of Acts. At the end of the chapter the disciples are commanded to
'stay here in the city until you have been clothed with power from on high'. On
the day the Spirit falls, Acts emphasizes that the early Christians are 'all together
in one place' (2.1).

Following the visit of the women to the empty tomb, there is the beginning of
a disagreement among the disciples. The women themselves believe. Many others
do not, and some investigate further. Before matters have reached a conclusion and
while they are in suspense, Cleopas and his companion reach the decision to leave
Jerusalem with their sadness, grief and questions. At the end of the story, despite the
late hour, they return again and the group is reunited. These are two travellers who,
at the beginning of the account, are heading in the wrong direction.

On the one hand, then, these two travellers are unknown disciples. They are not leaders in the community. They play no important part in the Gospel story or in Acts. What is more, at the point we meet them, they are breaking away from the main group, disillusioned and full of doubt. On the other hand, this is where we first see the risen Jesus in the Gospel of Luke. Does that not tell us something about priorities in the mind of Luke, in the life of the Church and, dare we say, in the mind of Christ?

Earlier in the Gospel, in chapter 15, Jesus tells three stories linked by a common theme: the parables of the lost sheep and the lost coin and the longer story of the lost son and his brother. The group of three stories is only found in Luke. They are told in response to the grumbling of the Pharisees and the scribes who say: 'This fellow welcomes sinners and eats with them' (Luke 15.2). Their common theme is the infinite value of that which is lost and Jesus begins with these words. 'Which one of you, having a hundred sheep and losing one of them, does not leave the ninety-nine in the wilderness and go after the one that is lost until he finds it?' (Luke 15.4).

On the day of resurrection, we see the risen Christ attempting to do exactly what the shepherd does in the parable. The main group of disciples is 'left' in Jerusalem. They do not yet know the truth of the resurrection. Jesus, as it were, takes all the time in the world walking unseen with those who do not yet recognize him.

There are a number of important lessons to be learned from this observation. The first is that the character and priorities of Jesus after the resurrection are exactly the same as during his life and ministry: in other words, the risen Jesus is concerned for the abandoned, the poor, the outcast, those who are far away from God and far from the community of faith. His love and his presence are not confined to the Christian community and to very holy people. His guidance and help are available to us especially in those times when we find ourselves on the edge of faith, in doubt and despair and wandering away (even though we may not be able to recognize him).

In the second place, the Emmaus disciples are able to recognize the risen Jesus and understand only because of the remarkable grace and gift of God. They are not searching for the risen Christ. They are not people of special merit or holiness: just the opposite. Like Saul's on the road to Damascus, their encounter with Jesus is unexpected and because of God's initiative. In similar ways, there is a sense in all our lives that we are Christians not because we set out to look for God, but because God set out to look for us and call us home.

And lastly, we should reflect that Jesus is here providing a model and example for the Church and for individual Christians: our priority also should be the lost – those who are outside the faith and those who are wandering away from faith. Those are the people who have the greatest call on our time and energy, care and compassion. As we shall see, Jesus provides us with some lessons in how to offer the invitation to faith.

I have gone astray like a lost sheep;
  seek out your servant,
   for I do not forget your commandments.

Psalm 119.176

Seeing Jesus

While they were talking and discussing, Jesus himself came near and went with them, but their eyes were kept from recognizing him (Luke 24.15-16).

Luke tells us in three different words that, as they walked along the Emmaus road, the disciples were 'talking with each other about all these things that had happened'. Later in the passage, he reports their conversation to us. The two companions puzzle to make sense of what they know so far. They recall different parts of the story as they walk. They ask questions about what it means. Like the women at the empty tomb, they are perplexed.

As they walk and share together, Jesus himself draws near. The risen Christ is present as his disciples meet together: 'For where two or three are gathered in my name, I am there among them' (Matthew 18.20). The style of this gentle drawing near is important. At the beginning of the journey and when the companions reach Emmaus, there is nothing forced or intrusive about Christ's presence. Jesus does nothing to persuade the disciples to turn round at any point. He simply walks with them and talks with them as faith and understanding slowly grow until they are complete. Everything else follows from this.

How is it that their eyes are kept from recognizing him? Different suggestions have been made. Some have argued that Jesus' physical appearance is somehow different following the resurrection, so that he needs to be identified in other ways by those whom he knew. There is a similar motif of recognition in some of the resurrection encounters in John's Gospel. Yet it is hard to argue for too great a difference here. It is more that, in this context, physical appearance is not the only factor in recognition. Some have argued that their eyes were prevented from seeing him by the devil but this goes beyond the evidence of the text. Others have said that God himself causes them not to see at this point. This is a curious interpretation in that the whole point of the passage is that the disciples eventually come to recognize the risen Christ.

As we have seen, Luke is exploring the truth that the way in which a person comes to see and recognize the risen Jesus involves a number of different elements. The disciples on the Emmaus road are unable to see because of (among other things) their sadness and grief, their preconceptions, and their lack of understanding, especially of the Scriptures. One by one on the walk to Emmaus, these obstacles are overcome and the picture begins to be clearer until finally, at the breaking of the bread, their eyes are opened and they are able to discern who Jesus is.

The main way in which Christians think about evangelism and sharing our faith is in terms of telling people something they do not know (the Christian gospel) in the hope that they will respond and change direction in the light of that knowledge. For that reason, the heart of the matter is seen as the effective communication of that knowledge through the spoken or written word. That picture of evangelism is certainly one part of Luke's understanding and occurs many times in Acts.

But the story of the Emmaus road gives a different and complementary picture. Evangelism is also about removing blindfolds and blinkers so that a person is able to recognize and to understand something that they can already 'see'. Jesus enters into the dialogue on the Emmaus road *because* the disciples are kept from recognizing him and in order that they will come to see.

It is possible to be part of a Christian church for many years as an adult and yet never come to a full and life-transforming faith in Christ. In order for that to happen, blindfolds need to be removed rather than new knowledge imparted. A teenager who has grown up as a child in Sunday school still needs to learn to 'see' and to understand and recognize that Jesus is risen, not through hearing the same message repeated or being told something new, but through blindfolds being removed and eyes being opened. Someone who has been outside the Church for all of their life can still have a deep and personal faith in God. Such a person does not need to be argued into the Christian community. He or she does need to be helped to 'see' and understand the place of the risen Christ within the faith they already have.

The Emmaus road story gives us some idea as to how that can happen, as we shall see, through dialogue, through friendship and patient listening, through honest rebuke, through seeing Scripture in different ways, through hospitality and in worship. All of these begin with the simple act of drawing alongside and walking in step with those who are outside the community of faith. As we ourselves explore the meaning of Easter, we should reflect on how often the risen Christ draws near to us with signs of grace and is unrecognized.

> Living Lord,
> unseen, you draw near to the first disciples,
> unknown, you promise to be present
> whenever two or three gather in your name:
> give us salve to anoint our eyes so that we may see[2]
> and rejoice in your presence all our days,
> for your glory and your kingdom's sake.
> Amen.

The power of listening

> And he said to them, 'What are you discussing with each other while you walk along?' They stood still, looking sad. Then one of them, whose name was Cleopas, answered him, 'Are you the only stranger in Jerusalem who does not know the things that have taken place there in these days?' He asked them, 'What things?' (Luke 24.17-19a).

Jesus begins the journey to Emmaus not with confrontation and teaching but by walking alongside and listening. He falls in step, attends to the ongoing conversation and then asks his first question: 'What are you discussing with each other while you walk along?'

The two companions assume that Jesus has been one of the many pilgrims to the Passover feast in Jerusalem and that he is now returning home or else to his lodgings for the night. They know he has heard at least part of the conversation and they are therefore amazed that he can have been in the city and yet not know what they are talking about. There is a moment of emotion and drama as they rest in their journey and reflect on their grief. Cleopas' first reply sounds brusque and angry. At this moment on their journey, the two travellers do not want to be disturbed by a stranger. Jesus has knocked on the door but it has not yet been opened. He knocks a second time with a second question: 'What things?'

This further enquiry provokes the longest speech in the story. The impression given is that, at the second time of asking, the whole sad story comes tumbling out. Assuming that the travellers continued their journey at this point, we should imagine that the disciples are talking and Jesus is listening for the first half of their walk to Emmaus.

It is hard to overestimate the simple, healing power of listening in any aspect of human life and relationships but especially in evangelism and teaching about the Christian faith. Again, 'listening' and 'evangelism' are not, perhaps, words that go easily together in the modern Christian mind. Our caricature of the evangelist is of someone who talks and smiles, not someone who listens and shows compassion, as Christ does here.

Yet listening is important both on the Emmaus road and for us to put into practice today, for at least three reasons. In the first place, through careful listening we learn what the agenda may be for the person we are talking to. We see the situation from their perspective, as Jesus does here. We come to understand what questions are uppermost in their minds, what they understand and what they do not, what point they have reached in their own discipleship. Some of the assumptions we have made about them are, doubtless, overturned. Others may well be confirmed. In that way, if we have opportunity to speak about our faith, we can know that the words we choose have at least a chance of being relevant to the person's situation.

Secondly, honest listening and the asking of questions, without intrusive prying, are the best way to establish a relationship, and the Christian faith is best shared naturally within a growing relationship of friendship and trust. Those who are on the way to faith need to know that Christianity is true, effective and worthwhile in the lives of people today if they are to be encouraged to explore the Way a little further. That is only possible if there is an opportunity to get to know other Christians and form friendships in a natural and unhurried way in conversations that engage in the real issues of life instead of staying on the surface.

Thirdly and last, listening provides one of the best ways in which blockages to faith can be overcome and blindfolds removed. The disciples on the Emmaus road have to trust Jesus with their questions and their grief before they are able to listen in turn to his response. Many people today are prevented from understanding or exploring Christian faith because of deeply rooted questions, anxieties, anger, grief, fear and hurt. There can be no engagement of the mind until these barriers have begun to be removed. This, in turn, cannot happen in most cases without careful and sustained listening. Talking about the grief or the questions in the context of faith is often enough in itself to enable people to move forwards. Most often, it will not be necessary to say anything in return by way of advice or counsel.

Jesus' question to the disciples on the Emmaus road is echoed by Philip as he runs beside the chariot of the Ethiopian eunuch: 'Do you understand what you are reading?' (Acts 8.30). It is unlikely that we will regularly come across people who are reading the book of Isaiah or thinking aloud about the death of Jesus. Yet, if we are alert, we may well discover people around us asking questions about the meaning of life, about human suffering and grief, about purpose, about Christian faith. When those moments come, they will usually be moments to listen, to ask gentle questions, to walk beside, before we venture to speak and bear witness to what God has done in Christ.

One final thought on Jesus the listener. The picture Luke gives us of the risen Jesus is one of the best guides we have to his character and nature, which does not change. In our own walk with Christ, we perhaps need to remember how well he loves to listen to whatever weighs heavily upon us.

Almighty and everlasting God,
you are always more ready to hear than we to pray
and to give more than either we desire or deserve:
pour down upon us the abundance of your mercy,
forgiving us those things of which our conscience is afraid
and giving us those good things which we are not
    worthy to ask
but through the merits and mediation
of Jesus Christ your Son our Lord,
who is alive and reigns with you,
in the unity of the Holy Spirit,
one God, now and for ever.

Common Worship: Collect for the Twelfth Sunday after Trinity

Hope disappointed

> They replied, 'The things about Jesus of Nazareth,
> who was a prophet mighty in deed and word before
> God and all the people, and how our chief priests and
> leaders handed him over to be condemned to death
> and crucified him. But we had hoped that he was the
> one to redeem Israel. Yes, and besides all this, it is now
> the third day since these things took place' (Luke
> 24.19b-21).

The two disciples on the Emmaus road tell their story to the stranger, not knowing that it is the stranger himself whose story they tell. The message they give is all the early Christian community would have had to say, if Christ had not been raised from the dead. As Luke tells the story, there is nothing inaccurate about their picture of Jesus as far as it goes. However, it is a picture that is wrong because it is simply incomplete.

The term 'prophet' is one that is commonly used by Jesus of himself in the Gospel of Luke.[3] The Gospel establishes that Jesus himself stands in the line of the great prophets of Israel, stretching back to Moses, the greatest of them all. Twice in the early preaching in Acts, Jesus is described as the fulfilment of Moses' own words that God would send another prophet to redeem his people:

> Moses said, 'The Lord your God will raise up for
> you from your own people a prophet like me. You
> must listen to whatever he tells you' (from Peter's
> sermon in Solomon's portico in Acts 3.22, quoting
> Deuteronomy 18.15).

> This is Moses who said to the Israelites, 'God will
> raise up a prophet for you from your own people as
> he raised me up' (from Stephen's speech before the
> council in Acts 7.37, quoting the same verse).

According to the Emmaus disciples, Jesus the prophet, like Moses, was 'mighty in deed and word before God and all the people'. The verse recalls the two distinctive features of Jesus' ministry. We have read of great works of power in which, like Moses, he fed the crowd and the sea obeyed, him and in which, like

Elijah, he healed the sick and raised the dead. We have read of teaching, parables and dialogue in which, like Moses, Jesus gives a new law and, like all the prophets, champions the poor and challenges those in authority. The same phrase, 'mighty in deed and word', is used of Moses in Acts and again echoes the language of Deuteronomy. Jesus' actions and character authenticate his words. His teaching interprets his deeds of power.

So far, so good. Yet now we come to the part the two disciples cannot understand. Jesus is a prophet, mighty in deed and word. He was the one to 'redeem Israel', to set the nation free as Moses had once led the people out of slavery in Egypt to freedom in the promised land. But before that could happen, as it seemed, 'our chief priests and leaders handed him over to be condemned to death and crucified him'. Two powerful pieces of evidence, Jesus' life and his death, cannot be reconciled. The one, as it were, seems to cancel out the other.

What is missing from the disciples' minds is an understanding of Jesus' death. At the moment it is simply a premature ending to a life of great promise. They cannot see in the Scriptures any reference to the death of this prophet whom God will send. They see no purpose in what took place on Friday in the place of the Skull. They look around them and see all too clearly that the Israelites are still enslaved and under Roman rule. Nothing has changed. Hope is disappointed and unfulfilled. Because they cannot see any meaning in Jesus' death, they are unable to perceive and believe the risen Christ.

As we travel with the disciples, we need to stand still and reflect at this point in the journey. We need to hear the disciples' dilemma in many views about Jesus expressed today. He is thought by many to be a good man; a wise teacher; mighty in word and deed. He is honoured by Islam as a prophet and by much of Judaism as a Rabbi or teacher. On such a view, Jesus' death is simply a premature, untimely and violent ending to the life of a good and gifted man. On this view, the cross has no meaning beyond the death of Jesus and the resurrection makes no sense whatsoever: it does not fit the frame of our understanding and therefore it cannot be seen.

And so we find also that to understand Easter and to comprehend the resurrection we must look back to the cross. The one cannot be understood without the other. This is not simply the story of a good teacher who died and came alive again and whom we can know today. There is a great drama of redemption taking place and to understand the plot at all we must understand the meaning of Jesus' death.

Lord Jesus Christ, we thank you
for all the benefits you have won for us,
for all the pains and insults you have borne for us.
Most merciful redeemer,
friend and brother,
may we know you more clearly,
love you more dearly,
and follow you more nearly,
day by day.
Amen.

From *The Alternative Service Book 1980*, p. 238

Hope awakened

Moreover, some women of our group astounded us.
They were at the tomb early this morning, and when
they did not find his body there, they came back and
told us that they had indeed seen a vision of angels
who said that he was alive. Some of those who were
with us went to the tomb and found it just as the
women had said; but they did not see him (Luke
24.22-24).

Grief, disappointment and questions live side by side in the disciples with the hope awakened by the events of the early morning. Through their retelling of the story we are reminded again of the story of the empty tomb. Jesus' death does not make any sense when set beside his life, promise and potential. The account of the empty tomb does not make sense when set beside the public death of Jesus which had been the talk of the city on Friday. How are these things to be reconciled and understood? We have returned again to the state of perplexity: old beliefs and uncertainties have been shaken. Jesus is the one who is to redeem Israel, isn't he? Death marks the end of our hope. Or does it? Out of this shaking of old beliefs and world views comes the possibility of seeing new things which we have not been able to see for many years.

Many of the resurrection appearances in the Gospels and Acts are meant to be seen as unique events for a particular time between Easter and Pentecost following Jesus' death. There is no way the encounter of Jesus with Mary in the garden or Peter at the lakeside or Paul on the Damascus road can find a parallel in ordinary

Christian experience down the ages. We remember the events as foundational for our faith. We learn and we move on with no expectation that we will somehow meet Jesus in the same way.

The encounter on the Emmaus road is, however, very different. Here the emphasis is not upon the resurrection of Jesus perceived through the physical senses of sight, hearing and touch. The resurrection of Jesus and the presence of the risen Lord are perceived and received, as it were, through two great channels of grace. The first is that of the word of God. As Jesus teaches them from Scripture, the disciples receive not only new understanding but a powerful sense of an inner encounter with Christ: 'Were not our hearts burning within us while he was talking to us on the road, while he was opening the scriptures to us?' (v. 32). The second is that of the breaking of bread, echoing both the Last Supper and the actions of the Eucharist: 'he took bread, blessed and broke it and gave it to them'. In terms of the story, everything about the risen Jesus is perceived through the breaking open of the word and the breaking of bread. There is no encounter in the story outside of these channels of grace.

Therefore, this story of the resurrection is different from all the others. We cannot expect to meet the risen Christ like Mary, Peter and Paul, through our senses. But the two channels of grace through which the Emmaus disciples perceive Jesus are available to every generation of Christians, together with the Holy Spirit dwelling in the lives of God's people and at work within the Church and the world. God has given us the means to encounter the risen Jesus as the Emmaus disciples did in the breaking open of the word of God. As we explore the things about Jesus in all the Scriptures we will discover that our hearts burn within us: our lives are touched at a level deeper than the mind. As we gather with God's people to take bread, bless and break it and give it to one another, we have the opportunity both to meet with and to receive Christ through faith.

As the disciples tell Jesus of their sorrows, their dilemmas and their perplexity, so we should remember that it is particularly at the times in our lives when things do not make sense that we need to come to God. Christians so easily fall into the trap of thinking that we have to present the best of ourselves to God: that we must have everything clear in our minds and think carefully about the words we use in prayer. In fact, the psalms and the prayers of the Bible teach us the exact opposite: our words when we pray are not supposed to be correct and orthodox and all worked out. They are meant to express our emotions, our dilemmas, our pain and our questions. Jesus' prayer of anguish in the garden is a prayer arising out of confusion and difficulty.

Part of living is to experience both joy and pain, faith and perplexity, often at the same time. The story of the Emmaus road teaches us that Christ is made known to us through the word of God and in the breaking of the bread both when hope is disappointed and when it is awakened. Meeting with God does not depend upon how we are feeling but upon his grace.

Living God,
your Son made himself known to his disciples
in the breaking of bread:
open the eyes of our faith,
that we may see him in all his redeeming work;
who is alive and reigns, now and for ever.
Amen.

Common Worship: Post Communion
for the Second Sunday of Easter

Guidelines for groups (2)

Sharing together (20 mins)

1. It may be appropriate for one or two people, or the whole group, to share something of their reflections from the time of prayer last week or from thinking about meeting the risen Christ in the time since you were last together.

2. Ask everyone to give their initial impressions from reading Luke 24.13-24 and the study material. If you can, share one thing you gained and one question you bring.

3. Describe your favourite walk to the group.

Studying together (60 mins)

1. Why do you think the two disciples are walking to Emmaus?

2. 'Their eyes were kept from recognizing him.' What is your understanding of how that happened?

3. Think of someone you know who you think needs blindfolds removed in order to come to faith or to grow in faith. Describe them to the rest of the group. How are those blindfolds likely to come off?

4. What did you learn from the passage about the character of the risen Jesus?

5. What did you learn about sharing faith with others?

Prayer together

1. Take time this week to plan an 'Emmaus walk' for the group. A 3- to 4-mile round trip is about right if people can manage that. If some members of the group are not able to walk then you can still do the exercise indoors, sitting down.

2. Divide the group into pairs. If there is an odd number, then one group can be a three.

3. Pray together as a whole group at the beginning of the walk (or commit the walk to God at this meeting if you are doing it separately).

4. For the first half of the walk one person should talk and the other should simply listen, without comment. What you talk about is entirely up to you: it may be a particular problem you are wrestling with, or an overview of what's going on in your life at present, or part of your story. The second person should simply listen, without any interruption, comment or advice. What is shared should be regarded as confidential. For the second half of the walk you should reverse the roles.

5. At the end of the journey, if you are able to, pray for one another and thank God for his presence with you.

6. When you next meet together, there will be an opportunity to talk together about the experience of being listened to by someone else in that way.

7. End your meeting together with a time of open prayer in a way that is appropriate for your group.

Chapter 3
Opening the Scriptures – Luke 24.25-27

The suffering and the glory

> Then he said to them, 'Oh, how foolish you are,
> and how slow of heart to believe all that the prophets
> have declared! Was it not necessary that the Messiah
> should suffer these things and then enter into his
> glory?' Then beginning with Moses and all the
> prophets, he interpreted to them the things about
> himself in all the scriptures (Luke 24.25-27).

In the second part of the walk to Emmaus, Jesus changes from listener to teacher. The pain of the disciples has been heard. The root of their perplexity is clear: it is impossible to reconcile their hope that Jesus is the Messiah with his death. Suffering and glory cannot go together. Their eyes are kept from recognizing him.

The opening rebuke should, perhaps, remind the disciples of Jesus' style. The strength of the language at this point in the story brings us up short and makes us think: are we, too, missing something? The heart of the matter is then caught in the central words of Jesus' speech: 'Was it not *necessary* that the Messiah should suffer these things and then enter into his glory?' The disciples, of course, cannot see that the two elements of suffering and glory are even remotely connected, let alone that these things were *necessary*. According to all the Gospel accounts, Jesus has attempted to teach the disciples these things before his death and to challenge their preconceptions of the Messiah. However, they have not been able to listen or understand. It was too much even to contemplate the possibility that the Messiah might be killed.

Therefore, now, following Jesus' death, it is important to revisit this question of the identity of the Messiah and the place of suffering within that identity. In a short time these and the other disciples will preach confidently to the whole world that the ministry of Jesus finds fulfilment in his death which was 'according to the definite plan and foreknowledge of God' (Acts 2.23).

Now on the Emmaus road, the risen Jesus demonstrates from Scripture that the disciples' understanding of the calling and person of the Messiah is wrong because it is incomplete and it is incomplete because there is no place for suffering. The exposition of Scripture is comprehensive and covers every section of the Hebrew Bible. It finds its echo in words spoken to all of the disciples at the end of the chapter (Luke 24.44).

Again we see the importance of the period of Easter in Luke's eyes. It is about far more than the disciples coming to believe that Jesus who was dead is now risen. It is about disciples who had been with Jesus and travelled with him at last coming to understand his significance in God's intentions for the world. In order to reach that point of understanding, the disciples must 'see' Jesus faithfully against the backdrop of 'all the scriptures'.

That calling remains important for the Church in every generation. It would have been a temptation for the early Gentile churches to pay very little attention to the Jewish Scriptures. They had their own writings about Jesus. Much of the Old Testament seemed obscure and difficult to understand. From time to time, false teachers rose up who wanted to cut Christianity off from its Jewish roots. This temptation was resisted by the Church as a whole because, from the apostles onwards, it was clear that it was impossible to understand the life, ministry, death and resurrection of Jesus apart from the Scriptures. For that reason, the New Testament documents are soaked in Old Testament Scriptures and use their language and imagery as well as around 2,500 identifiable allusions or quotations.

However, it was also very clear to the Early Church, that the task of *interpreting* the Scriptures was vital. It is not sufficient simply to read the text. The Scriptures must be read and interpreted with honesty and care as Jesus interprets them on the Emmaus road for the disciples. One of the central principles of Christian interpretation of Scripture has always been the one established here, that the Old Testament bears witness to the ministry, death and resurrection of Christ.

As the Church today engages in its call to make disciples, there is a great need to recover and to guard these two principles. Those who are new to faith and growing in faith need to be introduced to the whole of the Scriptures, including the part we know as the Old Testament. Without it, we are unable to reach a full understanding of Jesus. Secondly, those who are new to faith and growing in faith need to come to understand that the Scriptures need to be interpreted responsibly and with care for the good of the whole Church. This work of interpretation is central to Jesus' concerns on the Emmaus road.

Almighty Father,
who in your great mercy gladdened the disciples with
    the sight of the risen Lord:
give us such knowledge of his presence with us,
that we may be strengthened and sustained by his risen life
and serve you continually in righteousness and truth;
through Jesus Christ your Son our Lord,
who is alive and reigns with you,
in the unity of the Holy Spirit,
one God, now and for ever.
Amen.

Common Worship: Collect for the Third Sunday of Easter

My servant

Here is my servant, whom I uphold,
my chosen, in whom my soul delights;
I have put my spirit upon him;
he will bring forth justice to the nations.
He will not cry or lift up his voice,
or make it heard in the street;
a bruised reed he will not break,
and a dimly burning wick he will not quench;
he will faithfully bring forth justice.
He will not grow faint or be crushed
until he has established justice in the earth;
and the coastlands wait for his teaching (Isaiah 42.1-4).

Which passages of Scripture did Jesus quote to the two disciples on the walk to Emmaus? We know the tour was comprehensive, that it was detailed and that it centred on the suffering and the glory of the Messiah. It is, of course, impossible to reproduce. Yet Luke clearly does intend his readers to engage with some of the Old Testament as part of their reflection on the Easter story. We will therefore take our own more modest tour in this Chapter looking at passages from the Old Testament that we know are important to Luke and which therefore may well have formed part of the Bible study on the Emmaus road.

In the second half of the book of Isaiah, there are a small number of very striking and beautiful prophecies that draw a portrait of someone described by God as 'my servant'. The four 'servant songs' as they have come to be known, clearly played an important part in helping the Early Church to understand Jesus as the Messiah and especially in making the connection between suffering and glory. Words from the first song are quoted by Luke at the transfiguration ('my chosen', Luke 9.35) and by Mark and Matthew at Jesus' baptism (Mark 1.11; Matthew 3.17). As we shall see, when Philip comes upon the Ethiopian eunuch in his chariot, it is the last of these songs that is read and the gospel is preached 'starting with this scripture' (Acts 8.32-35). In all of the Gospels, Jesus describes himself frequently as a servant and links his ministry as a servant to his suffering and death:

> But it is not so among you; but whoever wishes to become great among you must be your servant, and whoever wishes to be first among you must be slave of all. For the Son of Man came not to be served but to serve, and to give his life a ransom for many (Mark 10.43-45).

> But I am among you as one who serves (Luke 22.27).

> And during supper Jesus, knowing that the Father had given all things into his hands, and that he had come from God and was going to God, got up from the table, took off his outer robe, and tied a towel around himself. Then he poured water into a basin and began to wash the disciples' feet and to wipe them with the towel that was tied around him (John 13.3-5).

This servant language did not form part of the traditional understanding of the Messiah for the Jews of Jesus' day or for the disciples. Most of the 'mainstream' prophecies about the Messiah are rooted in the Old Testament language about the coming king. Kings were anointed with oil at their coronation and the two words 'Messiah' and 'Christ' mean 'anointed' in the Hebrew and Greek languages. Jesus fulfils all of those prophecies, but to see him simply as the coming king is not enough. The passages about the servant in Isaiah formed an important part of Jesus' understanding of his own ministry.

The picture of the servant in Isaiah emerges itself from a period of great suffering and anguish in the Old Testament. This part of the book of Isaiah (chs 40 – 55) is normally ascribed to an unknown prophet, preaching towards the end of the period in which many of the Jewish nation were in exile in Babylon. The people have suffered the loss of their city, their king, their homes and their hope. Out of the darkness of suffering, the voice of the prophet comes as a voice of comfort, hope and restoration. In the crucible of exile, something new has been forged in Israel's vision of the future. The centre of their hope now is not simply the restoration of one nation but justice 'in the earth'. The person who will bring about that hope is no longer an all-conquering king who will enforce his rule on others, but a gentle servant, called and chosen by God, and now presented to the world:

> Here is my servant, whom I uphold,
> my chosen, in whom my soul delights;
> I have put my spirit upon him;
> he will bring forth justice to the nations.

Out of his own experience of suffering, the servant is gracious in dealing with the broken and those who are weak:

> He will not cry or lift up his voice,
> or make it heard in the street;
> a bruised reed he will not break,
> and a dimly burning wick he will not quench.

Already we see hints of qualities of suffering and perseverance in the servant which will become much clearer in the later songs:

> He will not grow faint or be crushed
> until he has established justice in the earth;
> and the coastlands wait for his teaching.

This is the picture of the Messiah that the risen Jesus begins to paint more clearly for the disciples on the Emmaus road: a servant who accomplishes more through suffering than can be gained through conquest; a Messiah who will change the whole earth.

> God of all comfort,
> we give you thanks for the gift of Jesus,
> your servant, in whom your soul delights.
> When we are like bruised reeds, you do not break us
> but restore us.
> When our lamps burn dimly, you do not quench us but
> revive us.

> Give us your people, like him, grace, gentleness and
>   strength,
> not to grow faint or be crushed
> until you have established justice in all the earth
> for the sake of your kingdom and your glory.
> Amen.

To the **ends of the earth**

> And now, the Lord says,
> who formed me in the womb to be his servant,
> to bring Jacob back to him,
> and that Israel might be gathered to him,
> for I am honoured in the sight of the Lord,
> and my God has become my strength —
> he says,
> 'It is too light a thing that you should be my servant
> to raise up the tribes of Jacob
> and to restore the survivors of Israel;
> I will give you as a light to the nations,
> that my salvation may reach to the ends of the earth'
> (Isaiah 49.5-6).

The portrait of the servant in Isaiah 49.1-7 forms the second 'servant song'. The focus here is upon the servant's mission. The breadth of vision is staggering. From the ashes of a defeated and demoralized nation, the prophet has faith to see the coming of the servant who will be 'a light to the nations, that my salvation may reach to the ends of the earth'. The very fabric of the prophecy is one of resurrection and hope.

In the first of the songs, God himself speaks and commends the servant. In the second, the words are in the mouth of the servant himself. It is easy to see how the early Christians applied the opening verses to Jesus: 'The Lord called me before I was born, while I was in my mother's womb he named me.' The picture is one of the servant being hidden away and revealed at the appropriate moment. In verse 3, the servant is called Israel: that is the personification and fulfilment of God's call to his people. In verse 5 the same servant is the means of bringing the rest of the nation back to God. Yet this is no simple song of triumph. As in the first song, we find a strong theme of suffering, frustration and despair:

> But I said, 'I have laboured in vain,
> I have spent my strength for nothing and vanity;
> yet surely my cause is with the Lord
> and my reward is with my God' (v. 4).

> Thus says the Lord,
> the Redeemer of Israel and his Holy One,
> to one deeply despised, abhorred by the nations,
> the slave of rulers . . . (v. 7).

The servant is to suffer, yet also to bring life and that new life is not for Israel only but for the whole world. Hopelessness and despair give way to greater vision:

> It is too light a thing that you should be my servant
> to raise up the tribes of Jacob
> and to restore the survivors of Israel;
> I will give you as a light to the nations,
> that my salvation may reach to the ends of the
> earth (v. 6).

Luke quotes this verse directly, applying it to Jesus, near the beginning and the end of his great double work. In the Song of Simeon, as the child Jesus is presented in the temple, we hear echoes of this prophecy from Isaiah and the vision of salvation in Christ being for all peoples:

> Master, now you are dismissing your servant in peace,
> according to your word;
> for my eyes have seen your salvation,
> which you have prepared in the presence of all peoples,
> a light for revelation to the Gentiles
> and for glory to your people Israel (Luke 2.29-32).

In Paul's final summary of his preaching to King Agrippa, again we hear the words of the prophecy:

> To this day I have had help from God, and so I stand
> here, testifying to both small and great, saying nothing
> but what the prophets and Moses said would take
> place: that the Messiah must suffer, and that, by being
> the first to rise from the dead, he would proclaim light
> both to our people and to the Gentiles (Acts 26.22-23).

As we read in Acts, the early Christians were gripped by the vision of Christ as the light for the whole world. In consequence, their most urgent task, under the commission of Christ, was to tell the good news 'to all nations' (Luke 24.47) and 'to the ends of the earth' (Acts 1.8). That same conviction about Jesus has continued to guide and inspire Christian people in every generation and has meant that the Christian faith has leapt across barriers of race, gender and culture to become a movement that has transformed human society and still continues to expand and to bring light to the nations today.

We cannot 'understand the things concerning himself in all the scriptures' without grasping this larger vision of the resurrection. The gospel of Christ is not for people in one time or location but for men, women and children of every generation and in every place. Through the humble obedience and suffering of the servant of God, there is new hope of glory for the entire world.

Lord Jesus Christ,
though deeply despised and abhorred by the nations
you have been lifted up to glory.
In times of frustration, grant us your hope,
in times when we have spent our strength,
    renew our zeal,
that we may proclaim you as light to the nations
and your salvation may reach to the ends of the earth.
Amen.

Humiliation and vindication

The Lord God has given me
the tongue of a teacher,
that I may know how to sustain
the weary with a word.
Morning by morning he wakens –
wakens my ear
to listen as those who are taught.
The Lord God has opened my ear,
and I was not rebellious,
I did not turn backwards.
I gave my back to those who struck me,
and my cheek to those who pulled out the beard;

I did not hide my face
from insult and spitting.
The Lord God helps me;
therefore I have not been disgraced;
therefore I have set my face like flint,
and I know that I shall not be put to shame;
he who vindicates me is near.
Who will contend with me?
Who are my adversaries?
Let them confront me.
Let us stand up together.
It is the Lord God who helps me;
who will declare me guilty? (Isaiah 50.4-9).

The opening verses of the third of the servant songs give a word portrait of the servant in a close relationship both with God and with other people. There is a concern for 'sustaining the weary' which echoes the passage about bruised reeds in the first song (and is itself echoed by Jesus in Matthew 11.28). Again, it is not hard to see a likeness of Jesus in the portrait both in respect of his careful listening to God and in his teaching ministry.

It is the suffering and humiliation of the servant that now come into greater focus in this and the final song. The picture of passive, obedient endurance in the face of torment is striking. The servant endures blows, beard pulling, insults and spitting. Although not quoted directly in the Gospels, the image is exactly the one given throughout the accounts of the trial and Passion of Jesus. According to Luke's account, Jesus is mocked, beaten, blindfolded and struck on the face and insulted by those who arrest him (22.63-5; 23.11, 16, 35-39). He is tried before the council, before Pilate and then before Herod but is silent throughout before finally being condemned at the request of the crowd. The prophets have indeed declared that it was necessary for the Messiah to suffer these things.

Most remarkably of all, even in this picture of innocent endurance of suffering, there is also the promise of vindication (vv. 7-9). Despite the way things seem, they will work out in the end. This song offers no glimpse of the way that will be, simply that the servant trusts in God for help and support. The ministry of Jesus, his prayer life, his Passion and his hope of resurrection are caught in a few brief verses of Scripture composed hundreds of years before his birth.

See, my servant shall prosper;
he shall be exalted and lifted up,
and shall be very high.
Just as there were many who were astonished at him
– so marred was his appearance, beyond human
semblance,
and his form beyond that of mortals –
so he shall startle many nations;
kings shall shut their mouths because of him;
for that which had not been told them they shall see,
and that which they had not heard they shall
contemplate (Isaiah 52.13-15).

If the first three servant songs give us a portrait in which we see the likeness of Jesus, the fourth is remarkable in its accuracy. It is the longest of the four pieces by far, continuing through the whole of Isaiah 53, and undoubtedly the best known. As we have seen, this is the song that is quoted to Philip by the Ethiopian eunuch in the passage in Acts which has many parallels with the Emmaus road story (Acts 8.26-40). If we can say with certainty that any passage featured in Jesus' teaching on the road to Emmaus, it would be this one.

The opening verses of the passage again stress both the glory of the servant ('prosper . . . be exalted . . . lifted up . . . shall be very high') and the suffering ('so marred was his appearance, beyond human semblance'). In fact, read carefully the passage is saying that the servant's glory shall be as great as his suffering has been deep. The nations and kings of the earth form the audience and backdrop to the great drama. Once again, the vision is a wide one. What is more, understood correctly, almost the whole of the following chapter should be understood as 'spoken' by the kings and nations of the earth astonished at what has been accomplished through the servant for their sake. Unlike the people of Israel who 'listen, but never understand' and 'look, but never perceive' (Isaiah 6.9; Acts 28.26), these kings and nations shall 'see' what has not been told them and 'contemplate' what they had not heard. It is their testimony which we are now invited to hear.

Lord God,
morning by morning, waken me,
waken my ear to listen as those who are taught.
Sustain by your word those who are weary,
strengthen those who suffer at the hands of others,
vindicate the oppressed,

and open the eyes of the nations to see your glory
in your servant, our Saviour, Jesus Christ.
Amen.

By his bruises we are healed

The main part of the fourth servant song is a Hebrew poem in four equal sections
of three verses each. Hebrew poetry works not through rhyme but through the
meaning of the words: normally the two halves of the verse complement one
another, with the second half saying the same thing as the first but slightly
differently. Remember as you read that this is intended to be a poetic description
of the servant, not a literal one.

It is unclear from the text itself what exactly the prophet is describing in terms
of the experience of his own day. The Ethiopian's question is still relevant today:
'About whom, may I ask you, does the prophet say this, about himself or about
about someone else?' (Acts 8.34). Undoubtedly the words are informed by the
suffering of the whole nation of Israel and probably the suffering of the prophet.
They also draw on the example of earlier prophets, especially the example of
Jeremiah, and on the psalms. Perhaps, in their context, they are words trying to
find meaning in the immense suffering of Israel. Even so, from the Gospel writers
onwards, Christians have found words here which not only describe the suffering
and glory of Jesus but, remarkably, help us to understand the meaning of his death
and the new life he gives.

> Who has believed what we have heard?
> And to whom has the arm of the Lord been revealed?
> For he grew up before him like a young plant,
> and like a root out of dry ground;
> he had no form or majesty that we should look at him,
> nothing in his appearance that we should desire him.
> He was despised and rejected by others;
> a man of suffering and acquainted with infirmity;
> and as one from whom others hide their faces
> he was despised, and we held him of no account
> (Isaiah 53.1-3).

The first movement of the poem is descriptive and tells us of the life of the servant,
through the eyes of the kings and the nations of 52.15. Again, to a large degree,
without forcing the text in any way, we see a portrait of Jesus who is born to

humble parents and lived most of his life in obscurity, yet whose name was known throughout the world within 30 years of his death and has been known throughout the world ever since. He was not famous for his looks, his wealth, his writings or the size of his following. He was rejected by at least some in his family, by those in his home town of Nazareth, by the leaders of his own people and the mob in Jerusalem. By both Romans and Jews he was despised and held of no account. He knew suffering well in all its forms: pain, isolation, grief and anguish. Yet what was that suffering for?

> Surely he has borne our infirmities
> and carried our diseases;
> yet we accounted him stricken,
> struck down by God, and afflicted.
> But he was wounded for our transgressions,
> crushed for our iniquities;
> upon him was the punishment that made us whole,
> and by his bruises we are healed.
> All we like sheep have gone astray;
> we have all turned to our own way,
> and the Lord has laid on him
> the iniquity of us all (Isaiah 53.4-6).

Part two of the poem offers an interpretation of the life and suffering described in part one. Seven times in three verses we read that the suffering is for 'our sake'. The speakers are still the kings and nations of the earth, speaking on behalf of the world. Our infirmities, diseases, transgressions and iniquities are set right. Through him we are made well, restored, redeemed, made whole, healed, brought back to the right pathway and forgiven. To win these benefits, the servant is stricken, afflicted, crushed, punished, bruised and made to carry the sin of the world. The picture is one of a great salvation won at a great cost. Every aspect of every part of our lives is made fully well through the servant's suffering.

> He was oppressed, and he was afflicted,
> yet he did not open his mouth;
> like a lamb that is led to the slaughter,
> and like a sheep that before its shearers is silent,
> so he did not open his mouth.
> By a perversion of justice he was taken away.
> Who could have imagined his future?
> For he was cut off from the land of the living,

> stricken for the transgression of my people.
> They made his grave with the wicked
> and his tomb with the rich,
> although he had done no violence,
> and there was no deceit in his mouth (Isaiah 53.7-9).

The third section of the song moves back to description. Here the kings and the nations sing not of the life of the servant but of his death. As in the third song, the servant is the innocent accused who is, moreover, silent in the face of his accusation and pain. Through a perversion of justice the one who is innocent is condemned to death and dies. His death and the manner of his death are as important in terms of the poem as his life and his suffering. The poem asks the same question as the Emmaus disciples: How can this be?

> Yet it was the will of the Lord to crush him with pain.
> When you make his life an offering for sin,
> he shall see his offspring, and shall prolong his days;
> through him the will of the Lord shall prosper.
> Out of his anguish he shall see light;
> he shall find satisfaction through his knowledge.
> The righteous one, my servant, shall make many
>   righteous,
> and he shall bear their iniquities.
> Therefore I will allot him a portion with the great,
> and he shall divide the spoil with the strong;
> because he poured out himself to death,
> and was numbered with the transgressors;
> yet he bore the sin of many,
> and made intercession for the transgressors
> (Isaiah 53.10-12).

And finally we move back to interpretation and to hope. The fourth movement interprets the third as the second has interpreted the first. There is further repetition of the theme of part two: the servant's suffering (and now his death) are for the benefit of others. His life is 'an offering for sin' (using the language of the sacrificial system).

> The righteous one . . . shall make many righteous, and
> he shall bear their iniquities (v. 11).

> he bore the sin of many, and made intercession for the
> transgressors (v. 12).

Clearly, the death of the servant is interpreted as a means to forgiveness of sins
for the nations of the earth. Yet this fourth section of the poem also sounds a
new note of hope and of new life:

> he shall see his offspring, and shall prolong his days
> (v. 10).

> Out of his anguish he shall see light (v. 11).

> Therefore I will allot him a portion with the great, and
> he shall divide the spoil with the strong (v. 12).

There is death here, but there is also resurrection expressed in the only language
the Old Testament has. There is suffering here for the servant of God, but there is
also glory.

> Lord Jesus Christ,
> you have borne my infirmities
> and carried my diseases.
> Through your death on the cross
> I am forgiven, cleansed, made whole and welcomed
>   home.
> Through your resurrection I have been given new life.
> As I have received the gospel,
> so give me grace to live it.
> Amen.

Therefore my heart was glad

> I saw the Lord always before me,
> for he is at my right hand so that I will not be shaken;
> therefore my heart was glad, and my tongue rejoiced;
> moreover, my flesh will live in hope.
> For you will not abandon my soul to Hades,
> or let your Holy One experience corruption.

> You have made known to me the ways of life;
> you will make me full of gladness with your presence
> (Acts 2.25-28, quoting Psalm 16.8-11).

Jesus' teaching on the Emmaus road is about new life and resurrection as well as suffering and death. The early Christians held to a firm conviction that Jesus was raised from death on the third day 'according to the scriptures' (1 Corinthians 15.4). It is therefore safe to assume that at least some of the passages discussed on the Emmaus road describe the Messiah entering his glory. Again, the New Testament writers draw on a range of texts. These verses from Psalm 16 have a special place. This is the passage that Peter uses on the day of Pentecost to demonstrate the resurrection of the Messiah:

> this man, handed over to you according to the definite
> plan and foreknowledge of God, you crucified and
> killed by the hands of those outside the law. But God
> raised him up, having freed him from death, because it
> was impossible for him to be held in its power. For
> David says concerning him . . . (Acts 2.23-25).

Peter's quotation is from the Greek translation of the Hebrew psalms, which accounts for some minor differences in wording between the Acts text and the translation of the psalm in an English Bible. In its context, the psalm is a song of trust and security addressed to God. There are a number of psalms of this type in the Psalter, of which the most famous is Psalm 23, 'The Lord is my shepherd'.

The Old Testament wrestles with the problem and question of death. On the whole, death is seen as an ending and an enemy, a descent into the nothingness of Sheol. There are various hints that life continues for some (such as Enoch or Elijah), but the basic picture is one of a life coming to an end at the grave and a general cry before God that this should not be so. Some of the psalms, like Psalm 16, express such faith and confidence in God to suggest that life does continue for ever. However, this in itself sharpens the problem, because, as Peter says, David and other kings who prayed these words had all died and their tombs were visible in Jerusalem.

And so the words become another unfulfilled (and largely unseen) prophecy about the coming king (or Christ or Messiah). He is the one who will conquer death. Jesus is the Son of David who is able to pray with integrity: 'you do not give me up to Sheol or let your faithful one see the pit' (Psalm 16.10) and 'I shall dwell in the house of the Lord my whole life long' (Psalm 23.6). He is risen from the dead 'according to the scriptures'. The Messiah must 'suffer these things and then enter into glory'.

For ourselves, a major part of appreciating and celebrating the resurrection of Jesus must be coming to a new understanding that in Christ, death has been defeated. The resurrection of Jesus is not simply about what happens to Jesus. A gateway to new and eternal life has been opened for all people in every generation. The Old Testament wrestling with death has been resolved. Death is still an enemy – but the enemy has been overcome and Christ extends to us an invitation to eternal life.

God of Life,
who for our redemption gave your only-begotten Son
    to the death of the cross,
and by his glorious resurrection
have delivered us from the power of our enemy:
grant us so to die daily to sin,
that we may evermore live with him the joy of his
    risen life;
through Jesus Christ our Lord.
Amen.

Common Worship: Post Communion for Easter Day

Guidelines for groups (3)

Sharing together (25 mins)

1. Talk together about your experience of the Emmaus walk. What did you gain from being listened to in that way by someone else? Did you draw any lessons for the way you listen to others? Were you aware of God's guidance or presence in any particular way?

2. Ask everyone to give their initial impressions from reading the Bible passages and the study material. If you can, share one thing you gained and one question you bring.

3. How familiar are you with the Old Testament? Has this week's study made you want to explore it further?

Studying together (45 mins)

1 What Bible passages do you think Jesus discussed with the disciples on the Emmaus road?

2. Can you see the gentle servant of Isaiah 40 – 55 in the Gospel portraits of Jesus and in the Emmaus road story?

3. Does your church have a vision for Christ as a light to all the nations? What can you do to make that vision brighter?

4 Jesus gives an example of passive resistance to suffering and persecution. Should this always be the way for Christians?

5. What is your response to the fourth song of Isaiah 53? How closely do you relate the words to Jesus?

6. How have you come to understand that Jesus has conquered death?

Prayer together

1. In your prayer together this week, focus on thanksgiving and praise to God for the death and resurrection of Jesus 'according to the scriptures'. Take some time to prepare for your prayers by writing some simple words of praise and thanksgiving, either individually or in pairs, that arise from this week's study material.

2. As previously, set the scene for your worship and allow the group to change gear. You may want to change the lighting or set up a visual focus for prayer.

3. Begin with a prayer asking the risen Lord to be present with you. Follow this with a time of quiet: either use silence or a quiet piece of music to allow hearts and minds to be still.

4. Ask each member of the group to read aloud one or two verses of Scripture that have become particularly important to you through your Bible study over the last week or previously. Leave some space for silence after each verse is read. It doesn't matter at all if the same verse is chosen by several different people.

5. After the readings, it may be helpful to sing together or use a piece of taped music. The song 'Hallelujah, my Father' works well with unaccompanied voices (the words are on p. 16)

6. After the music or song, allow space for the prayers or thanksgiving that group members have prepared.

7. End your time of worship with prayers for any concerns in the group and by saying the Lord's Prayer together.

Chapter Four
Eyes Opened – Luke 24.28-35

Grace and invitation

> 'As they came near the village to which they were
> going, he walked ahead as if he were going on. But
> they urged him strongly, saying, 'Stay with us, because
> it is almost evening and the day is now nearly over.'
> So he went in to stay with them. (Luke 24.28-29).

Jesus has listened and has taught them from the Scriptures. Despite their hearts
burning within them on the road, the disciples still do not understand. As yet
they still cannot see that the one who is walking and talking with them is the
risen Lord. And now, here is a mystery. The small group comes near to Emmaus,
the goal of the disciples' journey. Jesus has spent time walking this road with
them. His business with them cannot be finished: they have moved on in their
understanding but are not yet witnesses of the resurrection. Yet Jesus 'walked
ahead as if he were going on'. The familiar stranger does not presume to be
invited into the home of the two disciples despite all that has been shared.
The initiative rests with the two companions.

Again we see the grace of the risen Christ, just as at the beginning of the
story where the dialogue begins with Jesus asking an innocent question. Luke
describes for us in story form what happens when almighty God invites us into
a relationship and friendship with him. He does not command our obedience
but invites our love. The invitation is to become sons and daughters, not slaves.
Therefore it is always given in such a way that our freedom is protected and we
have a right to choose to go further or not:

> God will not intervene in such a way that would
> destroy the delicate harmony of our freedom: then we
> would cease to be human. Always he must reveal his
> love to us in a way that safeguards our ability to
> choose how we respond.[1]

The images of this verse are developed and echoed by other New Testament
writers, especially by the writings ascribed to the apostle John. One of the pictures

John's Gospel develops of the relationship between God and each Christian is that of God coming to 'abide' or dwell in the heart and life of each believer: 'Those who love me will keep my word, and my Father will love them, and we will come to them *and make our home with them*' (John 14.23).

The book of Revelation develops this theme further with the beautiful and gracious picture of the risen Christ knocking on the door of human lives and of the Christian community waiting to be invited inside: 'Listen! I am standing at the door, knocking; if you hear my voice and open the door, I will come in to you and eat with you, and you with me' (Revelation 3.20).

Jesus begins with the word 'Listen!' which suggests that the knocking in the picture may not be very loud or easily heard above the other noise around the home.

This moment in the Emmaus story and the development of the same picture in the other New Testament passages should make us pause and consider both our own relationship with Jesus and the way in which we bear witness to God's love.

In terms of our own relationship, we need to be reminded that the invitation to move on or go deeper in friendship with God or experience of his love needs to be made, as it were, from our side. We need to listen to the knocking at the door and open it. As the Church moves on through the Easter season to Pentecost, we begin to think about the promise and gift of the Holy Spirit. Many Christians and many parts of the Church urgently need to experience the deepening and renewing gift of the Spirit in many aspects of our lives. Yet God the Holy Spirit should never be seen as some kind of impersonal force that overrides our personality and gives us gifts whether we want them or not. The Spirit comes in new ways into the lives of those who ask him (Luke 11.13). The door must be opened from our side.

Secondly, as we seek to bear witness to God's love to others, the picture of Jesus arriving at Emmaus should remain in our minds. It's very easy in our enthusiasm to attempt to make people travel further than they are ready to go. As evangelists, we need to build in moments when we too walk ahead as if we are going on, leaving the initiative to those with whom we are travelling.

Almighty God,
whose Son Jesus Christ is the resurrection and the life:
raise us, who trust in him,
from the death of sin to the life of righteousness,
that we may seek those things which are above,
where he reigns with you
in the unity of the Holy Spirit,
one God, now and for ever.
Amen.

Common Worship: Collect for the Fourth Sunday of Easter

The breaking of the bread

When he was at the table with them, he took bread,
blessed and broke it, and gave it to them (Luke 24.30).

We reach the high point of the story. Jesus is made known to them in the breaking of the bread. The disciples have invited the stranger into their home, presumably to stay as it is now evening. The guest then becomes the host at the meal and in 'the breaking of the bread', his identity is made known.

At first sight, this might seem to be a case of recognition at last through a distinctive and familiar action but there is, of course, more to the story. The language of verse 30 echoes two earlier passages in Luke's Gospel. The first is the story of the feeding of the five thousand (which itself resonates with the Exodus theme of manna in the wilderness): 'And *taking* the five loaves and the two fish, he looked up to heaven, and *blessed* and *broke* them, and *gave* them to the disciples to set before the crowd' (Luke 9.16).

Notice that the same four verbs are used (the Greek word *eucharisto* is translated 'blessed' here and in Luke 24 and 'gave thanks' in Luke 22). In Luke's account of the Last Supper and the institution of Holy Communion, we see the same pattern and the same words: 'Then he *took* a loaf of bread, and when he had *given* thanks, he *broke* it and *gave* it to them, saying, "This is my body, which is given for you. Do this in remembrance of me"' (Luke 22.19).

Clearly Luke is describing something more at Emmaus than the simple giving of thanks before a meal. The story resonates with the language of the feeding of the multitude and the Last Supper and therefore is strongly linked to the meals Jesus shared with his disciples and to the early Christian shared meals which developed into the Eucharist or service of Holy Communion that we know today. The phrase 'the breaking of bread', used by the disciples to describe what happened at Emmaus, occurs several times in Acts as one of the distinctive activities of the early Christians:

> They devoted themselves to the apostles' teaching and fellowship, *to the breaking of bread* and the prayers (Acts 2.42).

> Day by day, as they spent much time together in the temple, *they broke bread* at home and ate their food with glad and generous hearts, praising God and having the goodwill of all the people (Acts 2.46).

> On the first day of the week, when we met to *break bread*, Paul was holding a discussion with them . . . Then Paul went upstairs, and after he had *broken bread* and eaten, he continued to converse with them until dawn (Acts 20.7,11).

> After he had said this, he *took* bread; and *giving thanks* to God in the presence of all, he *broke* it and began to eat. Then all of them were encouraged and took food for themselves (Acts 27.35-36).

For the disciples on the Emmaus road, discovering that Jesus is risen is about far more than learning something through the reading and interpretation of Scripture (although this is a vital part of the process). There is also here a moment of encounter with Jesus, set by Luke in the context of a shared meal and the breaking of bread. For Christians in every generation, Luke is saying, discovering that Jesus is risen means more than engaging with the message of the empty tomb and the promise of the Scriptures. There must be a sense today of encounter, of meeting with the risen Christ.

Where does that encounter take place? No doubt there are many and various ways. God's power cannot be limited. People themselves are very different. Moments of revelation and encounter with the risen Christ happen in solitude and in crowded places; in structured times of worship and in the wilderness; in times of great desolation and in times of joy. Yet there is also a particular place appointed for exactly this kind of encounter. As we have seen, Jesus and his disciples give a particular importance to meals together. At the Last Supper, Jesus gives particular actions within a meal a special meaning: he takes bread, gives thanks, breaks it and gives it to the disciples. He takes wine, gives thanks and gives it to them and commands, 'Do this in remembrance of me'. The breaking of bread or Lord's Supper becomes a central act of Christian worship from the earliest times. In the experience of generations of Christians and in a way we cannot understand, Christ is present and received through faith as bread and wine are shared. The encounter with the risen Christ at Emmaus in the breaking of the bread can be our experience today.

Lord Jesus Christ,
we thank you that in this wonderful sacrament
you have given us the memorial of your passion:
grant us so to reverence the sacred mysteries of your
    body and blood
that we may know within ourselves
and show forth in our lives
the fruits of your redemption;
for you are alive and reign with the Father
in the unity of the Holy Spirit,
one God, now and for ever.
Amen.

Common Worship: Collect for the Day of Thanksgiving for the
Institution of Holy Communion (Corpus Christi)

Recognition

Then their eyes were opened, and they recognized him;
and he vanished from their sight. They said to each
other, 'Were not our hearts burning within us while he
was talking to us on the road, while he was opening
the scriptures to us?' (Luke 24.31-32).

Three elements emerge as vitally important in the disciples coming to recognize the risen Christ. The first is fellowship and companionship. The stranger on the road invites them into friendship through being present, travelling in the same direction and quiet listening. The second is teaching from the Scriptures and engaging the mind and the heart: addressing the questions that the disciples are asking in a careful and systematic way. The third is a direct and personal encounter with the risen Christ in the breaking of the bread: a moment of clarity and recognition, a life-transforming moment of faith.

In terms of the story of the Emmaus road, all of these things happen within a single afternoon. In the context of the Gospel story as a whole, of course, they are happening over a much longer period of time. Jesus invites those who follow him into an experience of fellowship and community symbolized by the group of disciples moving from town to town in Galilee and on the road to Jerusalem. Those who will come and listen are taught through parables and stories, through allusions to the Scriptures, in a way that engages them and invites a response. In the midst of the teaching and fellowship there are powerful encounters with the living God, often through the signs, wonders and healings that Jesus does: after the miraculous catch of fish, Peter falls down at Jesus' knees saying 'Go away from me, Lord, for I am a sinful man!' (Luke 5.8).

In any journey to a living faith in Christ today, the same three elements are likely to be present. My own story of faith is one of growing up within the family of the local church. The offer of fellowship and friendship was undoubtedly what held me within the Christian community as a young teenager. Christian adults within the congregation cared enough about the young people growing up within the faith community to give up time and resources and open their homes to a group of six to ten young people. Looking back there was clearly a sense of their being willing to walk in the direction we wanted to go rather than imposing a particular agenda.

At a certain point in my own journey, there was a need to engage the mind and heart and, particularly, to be taught from Scripture. In my case, that began through religious studies lessons at school. A student teacher took my very sceptical class of adolescents through the evidence for the resurrection and the empty tomb. Despite myself, I was impressed enough to begin thinking about the faith I had grown up with as a child and was beginning to move away from. Through the youth group in the church, I was introduced to different ways of reading Scripture for myself. A process of enquiry was beginning.

Fellowship and learning, however, were not enough. There was a need to encounter the risen Christ. For me, that took place during a Diocesan Youth Weekend away (where fellowship and teaching were also part of the experience). At the Communion service on the Sunday morning, during the singing of Patrick Appleford's hymn, 'Living Lord', I experienced a moment of encounter with Christ and a simultaneous dedication of my own life to his service. I didn't fully understand the experience at the time and, almost 30 years later, cannot understand it fully now. In the language of the Emmaus road story, my eyes were opened and I recognized him. In the well-known words of John Wesley, my heart was strangely warmed. The moment was one of deeply personal encounter: the point at which the faith in which I had been nurtured from childhood became my own; the point at which the God I had 'heard about' for many years became known. It is hard to see how the encounter could have happened without the fellowship and teaching. But without some kind of personal encounter, it is hard to see how the fellowship and teaching could have borne fruit. What happened to the two disciples on the Emmaus road is something that cannot fully be expressed in human language: there is always an element of mystery. Yet it is an experience that can itself be recognized by Christian people in every generation.

Lord, Jesus Christ,
I would come to you
live my life for you,
Son of God;
all your commands I know are true,
Your many gifts will make me new:
into my life your power breaks through –
Living Lord![2]

Patrick Appleford
© 1960 Josef Weinberger Ltd.

Witness to the resurrection

That same hour they got up and returned to Jerusalem; and they found the eleven and their companions gathered together. They were saying, 'The Lord has risen indeed, and he has appeared to Simon!' Then they told what had happened on the road, and how he had been made known to them in the breaking of the bread (Luke 24.33-35).

At the beginning of the story, the two disciples have become separated from the main group and are leaving Jerusalem. They are downcast, dispirited, disappointed and full of doubt. But their experience of fellowship with Christ, learning from the Scriptures and encounter is transformative. By the end of the story, they have been turned around (the meaning of the term 'converted'). Their doubts, fears and preconceptions have been removed. Their questions have all been answered. Their eyes have been opened and Jesus has been made known to them in the breaking of the bread. Their lives now have new purpose and direction. As far as they know, they are the first and only witnesses of the resurrection.

This important news now needs to be shared without delay. It is late in the day and, no doubt, somewhat dangerous to travel. Yet nothing will hold them back. 'That same hour' they get up and retrace their steps to Jerusalem. They return, as it were, to the centre of the story in Luke 24 and the early part of Acts: to the community of disciples gathered with the eleven. For the first time that day, the disciples are 'all together in one place'.

The ironies in the story continue. When the Emmaus disciples reach Jerusalem, they find, of course, that the risen Jesus has been there before them. They enter the assembly to be witnesses, only to discover that the community witnesses to them: 'The Lord has risen indeed and has appeared to Simon.' Simon is, of course, present to confirm his testimony. Then they themselves are able to tell the story of what has happened to them on the road and how Jesus has been made known in the breaking of the bread.

The majority of disciples in the room have not yet encountered the risen Christ. They are still, no doubt, at various points of perplexity, doubt and confusion. The faith of the whole group has, of course, moved on from verse 11, when accounts of the resurrection seemed to be an idle tale, but it has not yet reached the point of encounter and commitment which Simon, Cleopas and his companion have reached. The testimony that is given within the assembly now plays an important role, preparing the way for the encounter between the whole group and the risen Christ that is described in the following verses.

In telling the story in this way, Luke gives us material for reflection on the way in which faith grows not only in individuals but within communities. The witness to the resurrection within this passage is not, as yet, to those outside the faith but to those within it and struggling with its implications. At the Last Supper, Simon was instructed by Jesus, 'when once you have turned back, strengthen your brothers' (Luke 22.32). The testimony to the risen Christ given in the assembly has exactly this effect.

In the same way, there is immense value within any Christian community in giving time and space to allow for the telling of our stories of faith and bearing witness to one another about the resurrection. This is one of the ways in which faith and discipleship can be helped to grow within the life of a church.

It is certainly possible to make time for this within public worship. I have been present at a large number of baptism and confirmation services where the candidates have had the opportunity to give a word of personal testimony to the gathered community. The effect has always been both to build up the community of faith and also to help family and friends who are present move on in their own journey.

However, the giving of personal testimony and the telling of stories can also happen very naturally in small groups: communities where we meet one another face to face, get to know one another at a deeper level and seek to build one another up in Christian faith and fellowship. Within any small group there will always be some people who, like Peter and the Emmaus disciples, are at a point in their journey where they are very sure of faith. There are likely to be others who, for different reasons, are perplexed, doubting or downcast. One of the purposes of the community is so that one group can encourage and build up the other and the whole Church grow in its faith and Christian maturity. We are called to bear witness to the resurrection within the Church as well as to those outside. One of the first fruits of the resurrection of Jesus is the building of community.

Living Lord,
you have called us to be part of your Church,
the community of those who believe:
help us faithfully to witness to one another
of the power of your resurrection,
to build one another up in faith
and to equip each other for Christian service
for the sake of your kingdom.
Amen.

Lessons on the Way (1): Listening and learning

> Then they told what had happened on the road . . .
> (Luke 24.35).

The word translated 'road' in this verse is translated elsewhere in Luke–Acts as 'the Way'. The phrase becomes one of the earliest and most common descriptions of the Christian life and faith, and is used in Acts before the term 'Christians' is coined. Saul travels to Damascus seeking any who 'belonged to the Way'. In Ephesus, there arises 'no little disturbance concerning the Way'. Paul testifies to persecuting 'this Way' before the Jewish crowds. Felix is described as 'well informed about the Way'.³ It is no accident that Luke uses the same term here as he describes how the disciples came to recognize the risen Christ during their journey. What lessons can we draw from the whole story about the way in which people come to faith today, the different stages of the journey and the responsibilities we have as members of the Church?

The principal lesson must be that coming to faith, when seen as a journey, must be seen as a process involving the whole person. The Emmaus story draws out a number of different parts to that journey. We have looked at these already from the perspective of the disciples on the road. At the end of the story, we need to go back and see them now more clearly from the perspective of Christ the evangelist and from the perspective of the Church as we seek to share our faith today.

The first part of the journey, from this viewpoint, is about being present with people who are moving in the wrong direction, about drawing alongside in quiet ways, about listening and forming friendships. In essence, it is about fulfilling the gospel commands to love our neighbour as ourselves, to care for the stranger and the outcast, to watch out for the vulnerable and needy within the community.

This is a role for each and every member of a church, not for a few specialists. Through the ministry of ordinary Christian people, there can be a Christian presence to listen, to care and to befriend in homes, schools, hospitals, workplaces, wherever there are relationships and community. It is not a role that requires any special training since it is primarily about being ourselves. But we do need to remind one another that this ministry is part of our calling to bear witness to Christ wherever we may be. We are nurtured and sustained in this Christian service through Christian worship and fellowship. We will often find a greater fruitfulness in this area of our lives if we are supported in prayer by other Christians.

As well as this individual ministry, Christians will often seek to act together in drawing alongside others and caring for them, acting either as a single congregation or as a group of churches. To that end, Christians in many places have established places of friendship and welcome within the community for the elderly, for parents with young children, for the unemployed, for young people, for asylum seekers, for those in particular need. Sometimes these will be permanent, well-established projects. At other times they will be single, low-key events. The 'goal' is to befriend and serve people for the sake of the kingdom of God rather than because of a hidden motive to witness to Christ. But these places and events can also become like the first part of the Emmaus road journey: a place where there can be gentle listening; where isolation, grief and sadness can be shared; where hard questions about life can be voiced. It is not necessary for those who come even to recognize why Christians offer this kind of service and befriending, any more than the Emmaus disciples recognized the risen Christ. The opportunities for Christian witness develop through listening, through the building of relationships and community, and through a willingness to engage with and talk about the deeper issues of life.

In the second part of the Emmaus journey, Jesus changes from being a listener and becomes a teacher, exploring the Scriptures about the suffering and glory of the Messiah. Growing in understanding is an essential part of growing in faith. In the same way, churches also need to provide opportunities for those who are interested in Christian faith to learn more. The learning will need to be set within a growing network of relationships. It will need to be geared to wherever people are on their journey. It will need to be systematic in exploring Christian faith.

Providing such opportunities for going further and learning about Christian faith will not be the calling of every Christian. Not everyone is gifted as an evangelist although some people at least will find they have the words and the opportunity to explain the Christian faith on an individual basis. But to provide such opportunities for learning is one of the primary responsibilities for each local church, and supporting these ventures in prayer, in practical ways and through welcoming those who come is a vital part of church membership.

Prayer suggestion

Take time to pray today for discernment about your own involvement in the ministry of listening and befriending, and the way in which that ministry is exercised within your home, work, church and leisure interests.

Pray also for the groups and individuals involved in teaching the faith to enquirers in your own congregation. If there are no such groups, talk to someone about setting them up.

Lessons on the Way (2): Encounter and witness

Listening and learning in the story are followed, as we have seen, by an encounter with the risen Christ in the breaking of the bread. There is no way of determining beforehand when or how such an encounter will take place for someone who has begun to learn about Christian faith within a small group or through the witness of other Christians. Every journey is different.

For some people, the road to faith will begin with a dramatic and powerful experience of God's grace, perhaps before they learn anything of the gospel at all. For others, there may be a gradual, slowly growing sense of God's presence over a period of several months or years rather than any dateable single event. Still others may be conscious of reaching a crossroads in their journey where they need to make a clear and definite decision to follow Christ. Others again may be given rich and life-changing experiences of the Holy Spirit on different occasions in their journey.

God deals with us as individuals, as he dealt differently with the women at the tomb, with Simon, with the disciples on the Emmaus road and with the remainder of the group in Jerusalem. We are wise to listen to and learn from the experiences of other people as they bear witness to us about the power of the resurrection in their own lives.

However, we are also wise not to take any one pattern or experience as somehow 'normal'. God loves variety and difference. What we should expect is that a journey to faith in Christ will involve *both* inner transformation as we meet with God in different ways *and* public declaration of faith through baptism, confirmation or being received into church membership. Nor should we think that an encounter with the risen Christ is only something that happens at the beginning of our Christian lives. Many Christians bear witness to a sense of growing friendship with God nurtured through private prayer, through Holy Communion, through drawing apart and through being actively engaged in ministry. Many Christians also testify to a pattern in their lives of both seeking and receiving God's renewing grace through the gift of the Holy Spirit.

The fourth and final movement in the story is that of Christian witness. The disciples cannot but speak of what they have seen and heard. For the present, their witness is confined to the community of faith. Within a matter of weeks, in the power of the Spirit, that witness will spill over into the community around in such a way that thousands of people are converted and the gospel is carried throughout the Roman Empire. We read in Acts of the message of the death and resurrection of Christ being proclaimed in every place to both Jews and Gentiles and turning the world upside down (Acts 17.6). This faith in the resurrection of Jesus was and is remarkably powerful and effective, crossing enormous cultural and geographical boundaries.

From the earliest days of the Church, men and women have been prepared both to give their lives in the service of this gospel (in the sense of dedicating all of their days and years to proclaiming it) and, literally, to die for their faith. The word 'martyr' is simply the Greek word for 'witness'. Acts describes those who are killed for their witness to the resurrection, beginning with Stephen in Acts 7. Christians have been so sure of the truth of their faith and the hope within them that they have been prepared to give up their lives for the sake of what is to come. It is a pattern which continues to this day as Christians are persecuted for their faith in different parts of the world.

Risen Lord,
unrecognized you walk with us,
you comfort our sorrows
and strengthen our understanding:
grant us a continual sense
of your presence on the Way,
that we may witness to the world
of the power of the resurrection,
for your glory's sake.
Amen.

Guidelines for groups (4)

Sharing together (25 mins)

1. Reflect together on your experience of prayer last time you met and in your own prayers recently. Are there good things you can share?

2. Ask everyone to give their initial impressions from reading the Bible passages and the study material. If you can, share one thing you gained and one question you bring.

3. Tell one another about a memorable experience of a service of Holy Communion.

Studying together (45 mins)

1. Can you think of other examples from the Gospels where Jesus waits to be invited? Can you think of any examples of the opposite characteristics?

2. Why do you think Luke places such emphasis on the disciples recognizing Jesus in the breaking of the bread?

3. When and how were your eyes opened to recognize Jesus?

4. Allow time for members of the group to tell the story of their own encounter with the risen Christ. What part was played by fellowship, understanding the Scriptures and encounter with Christ?

Prayer together

The most natural way to pray and worship together in this session is the context of a shared meal, remembering the meals Jesus shared with the disciples, the supper at Emmaus and the table fellowship which formed part of the experience of the Early Church. A certain amount of advance thought and planning will be needed. You could decide to use part of one of your gatherings for planning and the next meeting for the shared meal – or else plan in advance of this session and weave the different sections of the Bible study into the framework of a meal.

It will be important to distinguish clearly between this kind of shared meal and a service of Holy Communion (which, in the Church of England, requires an ordained priest to be present and an authorized liturgy to be used). In the order suggested here there is nothing equivalent to a eucharistic prayer said by a priest and no distribution of the elements of bread and wine.

The meal itself should be simple and easy to serve. Ideally, the whole group should share in different elements of the preparation, serving the food and clearing up together afterwards. Be aware that for some members of the group, sharing a meal with other people may be a new experience. In between the different parts of the meal there is opportunity for prayer of different kinds. If possible, different sections of the prayers should be led by different members of the group. The leader of each section is called the 'host' in the service order. This person may change for different parts of the service and need not be the 'owner' of the home where you meet.

The suggested order given below follows the shape of the first part of the service of Holy Communion in *Common Worship*. Different prayers and responses could be used as part of the meal, from *Common Worship* or from other resource books. Whether or not you sing will depend on the gifts available in the group.

Give some thought in advance to the layout of the room. If you are having the 'study' part of the meeting first, you will need a short break to prepare food and rearrange the room.

Permission is given to copy the following pages for use at group meetings.

Liturgy for a shared meal

Part One: The Gathering

The host welcomes the group to the meal in the name of the Lord Jesus.
A hymn or song may be sung.
There may be space for silence or quiet music, remembering the presence
of the Lord with his disciples.

Sentence of Scripture
'For where two or three are gathered in my name, I am there among them'
(Matthew 18.20).

Confession

Host: Jesus Christ, risen Master and triumphant Lord,
we come to you in sorrow for our sins,
and confess to you our weakness and unbelief.

We have lived by our own strength,
and not by the power of your resurrection.
In your mercy, forgive us.

All: **Lord, hear us and help us.**

Host: We have lived by the light of our own eyes,
as faithless and not believing.
In your mercy, forgive us.

All: **Lord, hear us and help us.**

Host: We have lived for this world alone,
and doubted our home in heaven.
In your mercy, forgive us.

All: **Lord, hear us and help us.**[4]

Host: May the God of all healing and forgiveness
draw us to himself
and cleanse us from all sins,
that we might behold the glory of his Son,
the Word made flesh,
Jesus Christ our Lord.

All: **Amen.**

Grace

The host or another member of the group gives thanks for the meal to come in
these or other appropriate words:

Host: Blessed are you,
               Lord God of all creation,
               through your goodness you have blessed us
               with the gifts of food and drink,
               with the gift of your Son, Jesus Christ,
               with the gift of Christian fellowship:
               as we enjoy these blessings of your creation,
               give us also the gift of thankful hearts,
               and make us always mindful of the needs of others.
               For your glory's sake.
All: **Amen.**

First course

The first part of the meal is now served and eaten. The host might suggest one of
the questions from the 'sharing together' section as a guide to conversation.

Part Two: The Ministry of the Word and the Prayers

The first part of the meal is cleared away.
A hymn or song may be sung.

The Scripture reading

Luke 24.28-35
The host may offer comments on the reading or introduce a time of open
discussion.

Prayers of thanksgiving

These or other appropriate prayers are said:

Host: We give you thanks and praise
               for the gospel we have received.
               Christ died for our sins: Alleluia!
All: **He is risen indeed! Alleluia!**

Host:	Death comes to all through Adam,
	and sin reigns for a time.
	New life without end comes through Christ,
	and he reigns for ever: Alleluia!
All:	**He is risen indeed! Alleluia!**

Host:	Death, where is your victory?
	Death, where is your sting?
	Death is swallowed up in victory –
	the victory you give us in Christ: Alleluia!
All:	**He is risen indeed! Alleluia!**

Host:	We have been crucified with Christ,
	and live his risen life,
	to praise you for ever with angels and archangels.
	Christ died for our sins: Alleluia!
All:	**He is risen indeed! Alleluia!**[5]

A hymn or song may be sung.

One or more members of the group may lead a time of intercession either using set prayers or following the custom of the group.

Second course

The second part of the meal is now served and eaten.

Discussion and conversation might focus around the Ministry of the Word.

Part Three: The Sharing of the Peace

The second part of the meal is cleared away.

A hymn or song may be sung.

Host:	The risen Jesus stood among the disciples and said: 'Peace be with you.'
	The peace of the Lord be always with you
All:	**And also with you.**
Host:	Let us offer one another a sign of God's peace.

The Peace is exchanged following the custom of the group.

If there are any particular needs, it may be appropriate to take time to pray briefly for particular situations and members of the group.

The final prayer is said together:

All: **Glory to God,**
Whose power at work among us
can do infinitely more
than all we can ask or conceive;
to him be glory in the Church and in Christ Jesus,
For ever and ever.
Amen.[6]

A hymn or song may be sung.

The third part of the meal
If there is a third part of the meal, it should be served at this point.

The whole group should share in some part of the washing up!

Chapter 5

The Lord is Risen! – Luke 24.36-53

Jesus himself stood among them

> While they were talking about this, Jesus himself stood
> among them and said to them, 'Peace be with you.'
> They were startled and terrified, and thought that they
> were seeing a ghost (Luke 24.36-37).

The story of the first day of Easter continues. The 'action' of this new scene flows
out of the end of the Emmaus road story. The disciples have been prepared for
what is to come. Their curiosity has been aroused by the empty tomb. No doubt
others made their way to the garden during the middle of the day. They have
heard the testimony of Peter and the companions on the road to Emmaus. Once
again, they are 'all together in one place', gathered, most probably, in the house
of the upper room where they shared the Last Supper. The minds of the disciples
have begun to grapple with the truth of resurrection. They are able to say to the
two from Emmaus: 'The Lord has risen indeed, and he has appeared to Simon!'
But they have only touched the edge of understanding a truth that will transform
the whole of their lives and change the entire world.

In this moment of unity, of witness, of the beginnings of Easter faith, Luke tells us,
'Jesus himself stood among them'. We are not told that he 'appeared to them' in
the room, simply that he stood among them. It is almost as if he has been there
for some time and, one by one, the disciples are able to see him. There are echoes
of the Emmaus story, although this time Jesus is clearly perceived through the
normal senses of the disciples and he does not vanish as soon as he is recognized.
Again, it is both a gentle and a dramatic moment of encounter. Luke tells the
story as if it is the most natural thing in the world for Jesus to be present when
his disciples meet together. His first words are of greeting and of calm: 'Peace
be with you.' They recall the words spoken to the storm on Lake Galilee (Mark
4.39) and the greeting to be given by the disciples as they enter a new house
(Luke 10.5).

Yet Luke is also careful in his description of the emotions of the disciples. It is
not the case that the risen Jesus was greeted with instant joy on the part of the

gathered company. The words used are in contrast to the calm of Jesus' presence: the group is both 'startled' and 'terrified'. Strong feelings are aroused. Even now, the disciples' minds simply cannot accept the empty tomb, the witness of others and the evidence of their own eyes. They can no longer deny that something has happened to Jesus. But their understanding turns to the only explanation they can find: that they are seeing a ghost rather than Jesus risen from the dead, and therefore they are afraid.

Once again, the way in which Luke tells the story of the resurrection alerts us to the enormous importance of the truth at the centre of the story. The implications of the resurrection of Jesus are simply staggering. We cannot take it in all at once. As with anything that is unfamiliar, our emotions run riot and our minds search for other explanations.

All of our life we are confronted by the certainty of death. Those we know and love are taken from us. We can no longer see them, touch them or talk with them. We face the scandal that the life of a human person with their unique character, experience, gifts and memories comes to an end. When someone close to us dies, we face the long and often lonely journey of bereavement, learning to let go of the person but hold on to their memory. As we ourselves grow older, the experience of bereavement is more frequent. We are more aware of the certainty that our own lives will come to an end. Must everything end in death?

The message of Easter Day has enormous consequences for every person who has ever lived. As Jesus appears to the disciples in the upper room, gently and graciously, he is announcing by his presence that death is not the last chapter in the story of human life. Death is real and often terrible. Loss and grief involve great suffering. But there is now the possibility of *resurrection*: of new life continuing beyond death in new and different ways. The resurrection of Jesus expands our horizon to eternity. We still grieve for those who have died, but we no longer grieve as those who have no hope. In Christ, we will be reunited for ever with those we have loved.

This hope of resurrection, in turn, makes us think in different ways about our life here and now. It is a soft, gentle, subversive song of life. The values of eternity are different from the values of the present. We have new and different purposes to our lives. Easter changes the world from black-and-white to colour. This is the centre of our faith.

And this is the truth that the group of disciples in the upper room are now beginning to grasp. As we have seen already with the women and on the road to Emmaus, understanding is not easy. When truth is so significant, it has to be explored like a mountain. It cannot be swallowed in a moment like a pill.

'Jesus himself stood among them and said to them, "Peace be with you."'

God our redeemer,
you have delivered us from the power of darkness
and brought us into the kingdom of your Son:
grant, that as by his death he has recalled us to life,
so by his continual presence in us he may raise us to
   eternal joy;
through Jesus Christ, your Son our Lord,
who is alive and reigns with you,
in the unity of the Holy Spirit,
one God, now and for ever.
Amen.

Common Worship: Collect for the Sixth Sunday of Easter

Doubt and demonstration

He said to them, 'Why are you frightened, and why do doubts arise in your hearts? Look at my hands and my feet; see that it is I myself. Touch me and see; for a ghost does not have flesh and bones as you see that I have.' And when he had said this, he showed them his hands and his feet. While in their joy they were disbelieving and still wondering, he said to them, 'Have you anything here to eat?' They gave him a piece of broiled fish, and he took it and ate in their presence (Luke 24.38-43).

Doubt and fear are the enemies of faith. In this passage, Jesus confronts both emotions in the disciples, preparing them for the mission that is to come. On the Emmaus road, Jesus begins with addressing the disciples at the level of their sadness, disappointment and confusion, so here he speaks to their emotions before he engages with their minds (vv. 44-49). Again, as in the Emmaus road story, we see the whole person is addressed, only here the order and the details are different:

The Emmaus road

1. Emotions of sadness and confusion are addressed through companionship and listening.

2. Mind and understanding are addressed through interpretation of the Scriptures.

3. The whole person is addressed through encounter in the breaking of the bread.

4. Jesus can no longer be seen.

5. Consequence: the disciples become witnesses of the resurrection.

6. There is joy in the assembly.

The Upper Room

1. The whole person is addressed through encounter and greeting.

2. Emotions of doubt and fear are addressed through physical evidence and reassurance.

3. Mind and understanding are addressed through interpretation of the Scriptures.

4. Commission: the disciples are to be bearers of the gospel and witnesses of 'these things'.

5. Jesus withdraws from them and is carried up into heaven.

6. There is joy in the assembly.

The encounter in the upper room is intended by Luke to be understood as unique and unrepeatable. The disciples encounter the risen Jesus physically in a way that is impossible for later generations. We must rely on the testimony and witness of the apostles, preserved in the Scriptures. By contrast, in the encounter on the Emmaus road, Jesus' presence is not perceived through the physical senses but in ways that are available to every Christian for all time: through fellowship, the Scriptures and the breaking of bread.

In the scene in the upper room, Jesus acknowledges the fear and doubt in the disciples. His question here should not be seen as condemning these emotions but he does go on to address them. Great emphasis is laid on the physical senses: the disciples are invited to 'look' at Jesus and to see especially his hands and his feet. Presumably this is because they bear the marks of crucifixion and therefore identify Jesus as the one who died and is risen. Hearing is involved as they listen to his words. Jesus invites the group to 'Touch me and see; for a ghost does not have flesh and bones . . .' The encounter is similar to that with Thomas described in the Gospel of John. Finally, there is a demonstration of resurrection through eating a piece of broiled fish. Again we are recalled to the meals Jesus shared with his disciples and to the miracle of the feeding of the five thousand.

During the encounter, the disciples move on in their understanding. In a fascinating verse, Luke attempts to capture a kind of halfway stage in their understanding, where joy, doubt and questioning exist side by side within their hearts and minds: 'While in their joy they were disbelieving and still wondering . . .'

Again, no doubt, Luke is attempting to describe the emotions of this group of disciples as faithfully as he can. Yet he is also drawing our attention to the mysterious process of conversion as it takes place within every Christian. It is not the work of a moment. We take three steps forwards then two back then one forwards again.

On Easter Day, the disciples 'believe that they believe' in the assembly when the two return from Emmaus. Jesus appears and, strangely, that belief gives way to doubt and fear. Jesus engages with their emotion and they are joyful, disbelieving and wondering at the same time. Finally, they reach a mature Easter faith and begin to understand what the resurrection of Jesus means enough to proclaim it to others.

Doubt and fear are common emotions in Christian people and those on the way to faith, especially in moments of great challenge, change and sensing a new call from God. We should not be afraid to admit to ourselves, to God or to other people that we are afraid or doubting. It is only when the emotions are acknowledged that they can be addressed. But while the Christian might often be called to pass through the place of doubt or fear, we must be careful not to make our home there. We are meant to move back to the way of faith.

Almighty God,
who through your only-begotten Son Jesus Christ
have overcome death and opened to us the gate of
    everlasting life:
grant that, as by your grace going before us you put
    into our minds good desires,
so by your continual help
we may bring them to good effect;
through Jesus Christ our risen Lord,
who is alive and reigns with you,
in the unity of the Holy Spirit,
one God, now and for ever.

Common Worship: Collect for the Fifth Sunday of Easter

Back to the Scriptures

Then he said to them, 'These are my words that
I spoke to you while I was still with you – that
everything written about me in the law of Moses,
the prophets, and the psalms must be fulfilled.'
Then he opened their minds to understand the
scriptures, and he said to them, 'Thus it is written,
that the Messiah is to suffer and to rise from the
dead on the third day' (Luke 24.44-46).

The themes of the earlier part of the chapter are repeated, underlined and brought together in this final encounter of Easter Day. The two men at the tomb recalled the women to the words of Jesus 'while he was still in Galilee' about his death and resurrection. Jesus himself pointed the two disciples on the Emmaus road to the testimony of 'the prophets' about the suffering and glory of Christ.

In this final Bible study with the whole group of disciples, Jesus reminds them again of 'my words . . . while I was still with you' and directs their attention to the prophecies about the Messiah in the whole of Hebrew Scripture, seen in its three parts of the law, the prophets and the psalms. The theme of the exposition is exactly the same as on the Emmaus road: 'Thus it is written, that the Messiah is to suffer and to rise from the dead on the third day.'

All through the last chapter of the Gospel, therefore, Luke places a very significant emphasis upon the Scriptures as the key to understanding and comprehending the resurrection of Jesus at the level of the mind as well as the emotions. If anything, the Scriptures receive an even greater emphasis before and after the Ascension than encounters with Jesus through 'appearances'. This emphasis should encourage us to take seriously the reading of Scripture today, both in private and in public. But it would be wrong to hear Luke's message simply as 'Read the Bible more often'. He is also saying something about how the Scripture is to be *understood*.

In the first place, he is saying that *Christ is at the centre* of the Scripture in every sense. That is easy to see in respect of the New Testament. Each of the books and letters is in some sense about Jesus and responding to his life, death and resurrection. But Luke is also making the very bold claim that Christ is also at the centre of the book we know as the Old Testament: the law, the prophets and the psalms. This claim is made in different and subtle ways throughout Luke's Gospel and Acts, but is focused and emphasized in this pivotal chapter. Jesus is the fulfilment of every strand of godly leadership in the Old Testament. He is the new Moses, yet greater than Moses. He is a prophet, but is greater than the prophets. He is the wisest of teachers, yet more than a teacher. Most of all, he is the fulfilment of the words and promises about the future king of Israel, preserved in the law, the prophets and, especially, the psalms. As we have seen, the testimony in the Old Testament about the one who will come, is understood by Jesus to be about both suffering and glory, death and resurrection. The whole of Scripture is shaped by this gospel message.

For this reason, the Christian Church has always been careful to see the Old Testament through the lens of the New Testament and of the gospel. At its most simple that means that when the Bible is read in public worship, the Old Testament and the New Testament are read together: the Old is fulfilled in the New, the New gives the principles of interpretation for the Old. It also means that we cannot simply quote passages from the Old Testament to one another and give them authority over the life of the Church today: everything in the Old Testament needs to be thought about and understood in the light of the life and teaching, death and resurrection of Jesus.

In the second place, through the way he tells the resurrection story, Luke is saying to us that *understanding Scripture is not always easy or straightforward*. That alone can be a great comfort when we come across something we cannot understand. The disciples were all familiar with the Jewish Scriptures but they are unable to see what is written there until Jesus points it out to them. We need help in reading the Bible, in understanding what is said and interpreting it to others.

Clearly, what we might regard as human education and learning can be very helpful here. Careful application to biblical study using commentaries and even language study will be helpful to any Christian, especially someone who is called to a ministry of teaching and preaching to others. Gifts of teaching and scholarship need to be honoured and respected within the Christian community. Those called to ordained ministry need to be encouraged to fulfil the promises made at their ordination to give time to study, and especially study of the Scriptures.

Yet Luke's third and final emphasis is also vital. Human skill and learning are important – but even with all the knowledge in the world we can miss the point entirely (and often do). *Christ is the interpreter of the Scriptures* according to Luke's account of the resurrection:

> *He interpreted* to them the things about himself in all
> the scriptures (Luke 24.27).

> Were not our hearts burning within us while *he was*
> *talking to us* on the road, while he *was opening* the
> scriptures to us? (Luke 24.32).

> Then *he opened their minds* to understand the
> scriptures (Luke 24.45).

Christ is the subject of each verb. Human understanding can take us so far, but beyond that point we need the help of God himself to open our minds to understand what is written. How should that affect the way we engage with the Bible?

Blessed Lord,
who caused all holy Scriptures to be written for
    our learning:
help us so to hear them,
to read, mark, learn and inwardly digest them
that, through patience, and the comfort of your
    holy word,
we may embrace and for ever hold fast the hope
    of everlasting life,

> which you have given us in our Saviour Jesus Christ,
> who is alive and reigns with you,
> in the unity of the Holy Spirit,
> one God, now and for ever.

Common Worship: The Collect for the Last Sunday after Trinity

The commission to preach

> and that repentance and forgiveness of sins is to be
> proclaimed in his name to all nations, beginning from
> Jerusalem. You are witness of these things (Luke
> 24.47-48).

So far, through the whole chapter, the focus has been on the disciples and their response to the resurrection. Now the emphasis changes. This message and its benefits are not for one small group of men and women but for the whole world. It is at this point that the Gospel begins to look forwards to Acts: the commission to be witnesses and the promise of power are both repeated in the opening verses of Luke's second book and form part of what binds the two volumes together.

How are the disciples to pass on what they have witnessed? The message is to be 'proclaimed'. The term used is linked to the word 'herald' – the one who would make public proclamation in a town or city of news for the whole population. The kinds of scenes envisaged are described in the Gospels (the public preaching of the Baptist who has the same message[1] and the public teaching of Jesus[2]) and also in the many scenes of public proclamation in Acts. The word should be a timely reminder to us of the need to announce the gospel in public places in every generation. Over recent decades, much of the Church has rediscovered the importance of evangelism that is friendship-based and personal. This is vital. But there is also a need for the more public 'announcing of good news' which the herald image describes.

What are the disciples to proclaim? As this verse and the preaching in Acts make clear, the content of the message is to be shaped by the death and resurrection of Jesus. Paul summarizes his preaching of the gospel in Corinth in this way: 'For I handed on to you as of first importance what I in turn had received: that Christ died for our sins in accordance with the scriptures, and that he was buried, and that he was raised on the third day in accordance with the scriptures' (1 Corinthians 15.3-4).

This is the heart of the gospel message as it is proclaimed throughout Acts by Peter, Philip, Stephen, Paul and all of the apostles.[3] It remains the heart of the gospel message in every generation. The gospel is good news because it is a message that leads to repentance and forgiveness of sins and therefore to new life with God. Again, we will see the apostles in Acts proclaim this message, invite the response of repentance and see many receive forgiveness. We are called to offer those around us a new beginning.

Where is this gospel to be preached? The vision is as large as it can be. The message is to go out to all the nations, beginning in Jerusalem. Drawing on the Old Testament tradition of Isaiah 49.6 and elsewhere, this is good news for the whole world for all time. It is also a message which Jerusalem itself needs to hear before it is proclaimed elsewhere. This order of proclamation will be given in more detail at the beginning of Acts and will shape the early part of that narrative.

The order of things as foreseen in much of the Old Testament is reversed. Many Old Testament passages foresee a day when the nations will come to Jerusalem to worship there. According to Luke, the risen Christ sees the activity of the Church not as inviting people to come to a particular place and worship but as actively going out and proclaiming a message in every place. Again there is a corrective to our contemporary understanding of evangelism. It is not just 'come and see' but also 'go and tell'.

Finally, *what is the role of the disciples?* 'You are witnesses of these things', says Jesus. There is a helpful distinction to be made between a witness and a herald. Not all of this group of disciples will be involved in public proclamation in Acts. That is a ministry to which only some are called. But all are called to be witnesses to what they have seen and heard and experienced of the risen Christ.

The witness of the apostles and this first group of disciples is unique in the history of the Church for they are eyewitnesses of the ministry, death and resurrection of Jesus. We should hear Jesus' words then as addressed to this group first of all and in a particular way. However, the call for all disciples to be witnesses is also addressed, through the Early Church, to every believer in every generation. There is still a need for the gospel to be proclaimed to all the nations. There is still a need for the whole Church to be united in witness to our own faith in Christ.

Lord Jesus Christ,
you call us to proclaim the gospel
and announce repentance and
forgiveness of sins
to all nations in your name:
enable your Church today
to be a faithful herald of good news
and a true witness to your resurrection,
for your glory's sake.
Amen.

Stay in the city

And see, I am sending upon you what my Father
promised; so stay here in the city until you have been
clothed with power from on high (Luke 24.49).

If we only had the Gospel of Matthew, we would be left thinking that after
Jesus gave the disciples the great commission, they simply came down from the
mountain and got on with the task. For Luke, there is another vital part of the
story to be understood and told in the Church in every generation. The disciples
are not commissioned to be heralds and witnesses simply in their own strength
but they are to receive the gift of the Spirit. For that reason, they must remain
in Jerusalem.

It is important to remember that Jesus himself received the gift of the Spirit,
empowering his ministry at the beginning of the Gospel accounts. According
to all the Gospels, he comes for baptism by John at the Jordan river and, in
Luke's words:

when Jesus also had been baptized and was praying,
the heaven was opened, and the Holy Spirit descended
upon him in bodily form like a dove. And a voice came
from heaven, 'You are my Son, the Beloved with you I
am well pleased' (Luke 3.21-22).

As Luke tells the story, Jesus himself ministers in the power of the Spirit (Luke 4.1,
14, etc.). The disciples are now to be equipped at Pentecost to minister in similar
ways. A central part of the testimony of Acts is that the effectiveness of the Early
Church in mission is due in large part to the empowering work of the Spirit.

Every good writer tries at the end of a chapter (or even at the end of a book) to leave the reader wanting to turn over the page, to keep reading in order to find out what happens. Verses 47 to 49 serve that purpose at the end of Luke's Gospel. There is a sense in which Luke is concluding the story of the ministry, death and resurrection of Jesus (as we shall see in the very last part of the chapter). But there is also a sense that questions are raised in our minds about what will happen to this group. Will the disciples stay in the city as Jesus has commanded? Will they be clothed with power from on high? Will the gospel be preached to all nations beginning in Jerusalem? For the answers to those questions we must wait for volume two.

Luke chooses to describe the Spirit in verse 49 in two different ways without using the term 'Holy Spirit'. 'What my Father promised' calls to mind the many Old Testament passages where the Spirit is promised to the whole people of God. In the Old Testament period, only a few special people in each generation receive the gift of the Spirit: they are prophets, priests, skilled craftsmen and kings. The coming of the Spirit upon such people is clear and identified sometimes through their experience at that moment in time but always through the fruit of their different gifts. However, in many places, the prophets foretell a moment when the spirit of God will be poured out upon all peoples. The best-known prophecy was that of Joel, quoted by Peter on the day of Pentecost:

> In the last days it will be, God declares,
> that I will pour out my Spirit upon all flesh,
> and your sons and your daughters shall prophesy,
> and your young men shall see visions,
> and your old men shall dream dreams.
> Even upon my slaves, both men and women,
> in those days I will pour our my Spirit;
> and they shall prophesy.
> (Joel 2.28-30; Acts 2.17-18)

The gift of the Spirit is also described in Luke 24 as being clothed with 'power from on high'. The Greek word used for power is *dynamis* – the word from which we take the term 'dynamite'. It is hard to read the early chapters of Acts and not think in terms of the explosive power of the gospel as it begins to shake the foundations of Judaism and of the Roman world.

What of the Church in our day? If the disciples needed to be clothed with power from on high in order to fulfil the commission to be witnesses, how much more do we! A careful reading of Luke's Gospel and Acts demonstrates that the empowering gift of the Spirit is not to be seen as a once and for all event in the life of the Church or the life of an individual Christian. The disciples have already experienced sharing the gospel in the power of the Spirit in the early missions in Galilee. They will receive the gift of the Spirit in a particular way on the day of Pentecost, but then be filled with the Spirit again after they have prayed together in Acts 4. In the same way, both the Church and individual disciples today need seasons in our Christian lives when we are renewed for mission in the power of the Spirit.

The key to those seasons is the command Jesus gives to the disciples here: 'Stay or wait . . .' For the disciples, waiting for the gift of the Spirit at Pentecost was not about when the gift would be given. It is not as if the Spirit had a long journey to arrive in Jerusalem and that waiting for the gift was like waiting for a bus or a birthday. Waiting in this sense is much more about preparation: understanding the cross and resurrection in deeper ways; setting relationships right within the community; becoming aware of the enormous task before them; asking God for the gift of the Spirit. Waiting is not always easy – but it is important.

As we come near to the end of this reflection on the Easter story as Luke tells it, we too need to hear again the commission to be witnesses. As we hear that commission, we realize that this is something we are unable to do in our own strength. Jesus' command to 'wait in the city' is not only for the first disciples but for every generation of Christians – including ourselves. As we have understood the resurrection in a deeper way, so we need to ask God for a greater outpouring of the Promise of the Father, empowering the Church for mission.

Prayers for renewal in the power of the Spirit

Come, Holy Spirit.

Breathe on me, breath of God
Fill me with life anew,
That I may love what thou dost love,
And do what thou dost do.[4]

Come, Holy Ghost, our souls inspire,
And lighten with celestial fire:
Thou the anointing Spirit art
Who dost Thy sevenfold gifts impart.[5]

> O Thou who camest from above
> the pure, celestial fire to impart,
> kindle a flame of sacred love
> on the mean altar of my heart.[6]

These prayers are best said slowly and repeated in times of quiet and waiting.

The end and the beginning

> Then he led them out as far as Bethany, and, lifting
> up his hands, he blessed them. While he was blessing
> them, he withdrew from them and was carried up into
> heaven. And they worshipped him, and returned to
> Jerusalem with great joy; and they were continually
> in the temple blessing God. (Luke 24.50-53).

We have come to the end of Luke's account of the new day of resurrection.
We began the day with the women taking spices to an empty tomb in the early
dawn. In the middle of the day we walked the Emmaus road with Cleopas and
his companion and with the risen Christ. In the evening we have gathered with
the whole community of disciples in the upper room as they meet the risen Christ,
receive instruction from the Scriptures and hear Jesus' final words in the gospel
of commission and the promise of the Spirit's power. Through the day the disciples
have moved on in their understanding of the resurrection of Jesus from mockery
and unbelief, to curiosity, to uncertain faith based on the testimony of others;
through doubt and fear and joyful wonder to personal faith and renewed
understanding of the risen Christ. We have seen the part played by physical
evidence, the testimony of others, listening and fellowship, the interpretation
of Scripture, the breaking of bread and encounter.

Now, late at night, the group of disciples leave with Jesus and walk out to Bethany
where he will leave them at the end of the day. This is the place where the Passion
story began (Luke 19.29). At Bethany, Jesus blesses the disciples and, in the
moment of blessing them, he withdraws from them and is taken into heaven.
Luke intentionally recalls a number of farewell scenes in the Old Testament and
in Jewish writings.

We read at the beginning of Acts that Jesus appeared to his disciples over 40 days
after the day of resurrection and spoke of the kingdom of God. After that 40-day
period, in a similar but different scene on the Mount of Olives 'a cloud took him

out of their sight' (Acts 1.9). In order to draw the Gospel to an appropriate ending, Luke seems to have brought together the scene in which Jesus parted from the disciples on the first Easter Day with some elements of the Ascension scene which he is to describe in more detail in Acts. The whole of Jesus' teaching in the period from the resurrection to the Ascension is therefore focused in the summary in the upper room: the suffering and the resurrection of the Messiah; the command to preach the gospel message to all nations; the promise of the Spirit.

The response of the disciples when Jesus withdraws from them and is carried up into heaven is no longer one of grief or sadness or confusion or doubt. It is one of worship.[7] In the final verses of the Gospel, men and women recognize Jesus as worthy of our praise and worship, as God the Son. The whole gospel story as Luke has told it has been about the way in which we recognize and understand who Jesus is.

In the final verses of the chapter, we see new horizons still for our understanding of the resurrection. It is a good moment to summarize the ground covered so far.

> We have seen something of the implications for our understanding of Jesus' death. Because Jesus is risen, then we are able to understand that his death was not a failure and the premature ending of his life.

> We have seen something of the connection between suffering and glory. One is deeply related to the other in Scripture, in the ministry of Jesus and in our own lives. The path to glory and resurrection is often through pain and difficulty.

> Because of the resurrection, we are able to see Jesus' death as significant and full of meaning for the whole world. Because Jesus died and rose again there is the possibility of repentance and forgiveness of sins for all the nations.

> Because of the way Luke tells the story of the resurrection, we can see the continuity between the character of the risen Jesus and the character of Jesus in the Gospels: gracious, gentle, patient, willing both to listen and to teach.

> Because of the actual, bodily resurrection of Jesus, we are able to believe with confidence that death has been overcome. Death is no longer just an ending. There is the offer and the possibility of new and eternal life with God.

> As Luke has shaped his narrative, we have been able to see more clearly the way the risen Christ is still present with his disciples today, even in times of sadness, doubt and fear, and the way in which we encounter his presence in Christian fellowship, in Scripture and the breaking of the bread.

> Because of Jesus' teaching in the chapter, we are able to see that the death and resurrection of Christ is the key to understanding and opening the Scriptures.

> Because the message of the resurrection is of such enormous importance to the world, we are able to hear in a new way the commission of Jesus that this message must be proclaimed in his name to all nations and that we ourselves need to be clothed with power from on high.

> Finally, we see in the disciples' response of worship, that the message of the resurrection has profound consequences for the way in which we see Jesus. He is worthy of our worship. He is the Son of God.

The response is one of praise. As Jesus withdrew from the disciples while he was blessing them, so the disciples respond through being continually in the temple, blessing God. The grace and goodness of God revealed in Christ result in a new rhythm for human life of both worship and mission, praise and service.

The Gospel of Luke ends as it began, in the temple in Jerusalem, with the first community of Christians caught up in worship and waiting for the gift of the Spirit. We turn over the page and wait for the next chapter to begin.

> Grant, we pray, almighty God,
> that as we believe your only-begotten Son our Lord
>   Jesus Christ
> to have ascended into the heavens,
> so we in heart and mind may also ascend
> and with him continually dwell;
> who is alive and reigns with you,
> in the unity of the Holy Spirit,
> one God, now and for ever.

Common Worship: Collect for Ascension Day

Guidelines for groups (5)

Sharing together (20 mins)

1. Reflect together on your experience of the shared meal together. Are there good things you can share?

2. Ask everyone to give their initial impressions from reading the Bible passages and the study material. If you can, share one thing you gained and one question you bring.

3. Talk a little about what you have gained from this series of studies and how you want to move on both individually and as a group.

Studying together (45 mins)

1. Look again at the sequence of emotions, understanding and faith in the disciples. Can you find each stage again in the chapter? Can you find each stage in your own life?

   - Mockery and unbelief
   - Curiosity
   - Faith based on the testimony of others
   - Doubt and fear
   - Joyful, unbelieving wonder
   - Personal faith
   - Call to service
   - Renewed understanding of the risen Christ.

2. What have you learned from this study and the series about the way in which Christians should read Scripture?

3. Are you called to be a herald or a witness? What have you learned from the chapter about fulfilling your calling?

4. The truth about the resurrection is like a mountain to be explored not a pill to be taken. Do you agree? Look again at the summary

of resurrection truth (pp. 92–3). Can you link each one to Luke 24? Which have you learned most about during this series of studies?

Prayer together

Focus your prayer together in this session around Jesus' words: 'stay here in the city until you have been clothed with power from on high' (Luke 24.49).

You may be able to find a way to do this which is appropriate to your group and situation – but here are some ideas to guide you.

As on previous occasions, take a short break after the study time. Rearrange the room and set up a visual focus for prayer, such as a cross, candles or some other symbol of the Holy Spirit.

Begin with a time of worship and thanksgiving. Use songs if you can – but also leave space for spoken praise. Invite members of the group to give thanks for God's grace and goodness around the themes of Luke 24. It may help the group to adopt an 'open posture' physically (such as sitting with palms outstretched and facing upwards) rather than the usual 'shampoo position' for prayer.

Read Luke 24.44-49.

Keep a time of quiet together. Members of the group should pray individually for the renewing power of the Spirit for their witness to Christ. You may want to do this in silence; or silence interspersed with short prayers or songs; or else play some quiet music to focus your own prayers.

At the end of the time of silence allow a space for open prayer.

Invite any members of the group who would like to receive prayer for renewal in the power of the Spirit to stand. The group convenors, together with those on each side of the person, should lay hands upon their head or shoulders and pray simply for each person in these or other suitable words:

> Lord Jesus Christ,
> we pray that you would clothe your servant N.
> with power from on high
> to witness to your gospel.

Be aware that God may answer your prayers in obvious or hidden ways; the 'answer' may be evident immediately or over the coming weeks.

After you have prayed for everyone who responds to the invitation, end the meeting with a time of worship using spoken praise (by saying a psalm together) or with songs.

Liturgical Resources

This section suggests ways of incorporating the study material into the Ministry of the Word as the congregation gathers on Sundays or during the week. A short series of sermons is envisaged, one for each chapter.

If the material is used during the Easter Season, the *Revised Common Lectionary* guidelines do not permit the substitution of alternative readings for Church of England services. The Emmaus road story is the set Gospel at the Principal Service on the Third Sunday of Easter, Year A. Luke 24.44-53 is the Gospel set for Ascension Day. Otherwise, RCL gives a high priority to John 14 – 21 in the Easter season in all three years. However, all the set readings allow for preaching on the theme of the resurrection, which will link in with the broad theme of the study.

If you are using the material in Ordinary Time, or you are able to adapt the lectionary provision for your own church, we have provided a table of readings and very brief comments linked to material in the Church of England's *Common Worship*. Music with an Easter theme is generally well indexed in resource material and so we have not provided any particular suggestions for that part of worship.

Chapter 1: The First Day – Luke 24.1-12
The Ministry of the Word

Isaiah 25.6-9
Psalm 16
1 Corinthians 15.1-11
Luke 24.1-12

The passage from Isaiah is part of the lectionary provision for Easter Day (Year B) and is a striking prophecy that the Lord will destroy death, 'the shroud that is cast over all peoples' on Mount Zion. Psalm 16 is the resurrection psalm quoted in Peter's sermon in Acts 2. 1 Corinthians 15 is the earliest New Testament account of the resurrection.

Other material

Throughout the series, the prayers provided in the text might be used as additional collects or post-Communion prayers or incorporated into the intercessions. The seasonal material for Easter in *Common Worship* is clearly suitable for the theme, even when the series is outside of the Easter season.

Themes for the intercession might include thanksgiving and prayers for the ministry of women in the life of the Church; and prayers for those whose witness is misunderstood and who find it hard to believe.

Chapter Two: Beginning the Journey – Luke 24.13-24
The Ministry of the Word

Genesis 18.1-15
Psalm 121
Hebrews 13.1-8
Luke 24.13-24

The Genesis story about Abraham entertaining three visitors at Mamre is another story about the Lord visiting those who do not recognize him immediately. The Hebrews reading comments on those 'who have entertained angels without knowing it' and speaks of Jesus Christ, the same yesterday, today and forever. The psalm is one sung by pilgrims on the way to Jerusalem.

Other material

The prayers should include an appropriate time of silence, emphasizing the theme of Christ as one who listens. The service may also be an appropriate time to offer prayer ministry following Holy Communion.

The intercessions could include opportunity to pray for those who are on the edge of faith, both those who are moving in and those who are drifting away. It would also be good to pray for projects and areas of ministry that build the interface between the church and the wider community.

Chapter 3: Opening the Scriptures – Luke 24.25-27
The Ministry of the Word

Isaiah 53.1-12
Psalm 19
Acts 2.22-36
Luke 24.25-27

The fourth of the servant songs provides the Old Testament reading, giving some of the content to Jesus' exposition of Scriptures and, possibly, the central passage for the sermon. Psalm 19 is a song in praise of the perfect law of God. The reading from Acts is part of Peter's sermon on the day of Pentecost and describes the way in which the Early Church went on to proclaim the death and resurrection of Jesus 'according to the Scriptures'.

Other material
The intercessions may well include opportunity for weaving together the themes of suffering and glory. Because of the emphasis on redemption in Isaiah 53, it may be appropriate to have the prayers of confession after the Ministry of the Word.

The authorized declaration of faith based on 1 Corinthians 15 (*Common Worship*, p. 147) might be used appropriately on this or other Sundays.

Chapter 4: Eyes Opened – Luke 24.38-45
The Ministry of the Word

Isaiah 55.1-11
Psalm 24
Acts 8.26-40
Luke 24.38-45

The Isaiah reading links to the themes of the Emmaus road story in a number of ways: there is an invitation from God to come and eat, which recalls the supper at Emmaus; a prophecy of nations being 'called' through Israel and an emphasis on the word of God. Psalm 24 is a psalm about the Lord's entry to the temple, one of the roots of the imagery of Christ coming to dwell in the heart of the believer. The passage in Acts 8 shares many themes with the Emmaus road story, especially the revelation of Christ through the Scriptures.

Other material

The prayers of intercession could include opportunity for quiet prayer for Christ to come and dwell within, perhaps in response to the sermon and in preparation for communion. There is opportunity to teach about the Eucharist and to give the congregation help in preparation to receive communion and in giving thanks through quiet prayer and worship.

Chapter 5: The Lord is Risen! – Luke 24.36-53

The Ministry of the Word

Ezekiel 37.1-14
Psalm 47
Ephesians 4.1-13
Luke 24.36-53

The prophecy of Ezekiel looks forwards to Pentecost and the gift of the Spirit. Psalm 47 is the psalm set for Ascension Day. The reading from Ephesians 4 makes explicit the connection between the Ascension of Christ and the gift of the Spirit.

Other material

A service based around the end of Luke's Gospel needs to look both backwards and forwards in terms of the commission to bear witness and the promise of the Spirit. These should form the themes for the intercessions with a particular emphasis on the witness of the Church to the risen Christ.

Notes

CHAPTER 1

1. 'Hallelujah, my Father', from *Mission Praise*, compiled by Peter Horrobin and Greg Leavers, Marshall Pickering, 1990 (Combined Words edition, no. 206).

CHAPTER 2

1. See I. Howard Marshall, *The Gospel of Luke*, Paternoster Press, 1978, p. 894.
2. From Revelation 3.18.
3. Luke 4.24; 6.23; 7.16, 39; 13.33-34.

CHAPTER 4

1. From *Emmaus: The Way of Faith: Introduction*, 2nd edition, Church House Publishing, 2001, p. 32.
2. 'Living Lord' from *Mission Praise*, compiled by Peter Horrobin and Greg Leavers, Marshall Pickering, 1990 (Combined Words edition, no. 435).
3. See Acts 9.2; 19.23; 22.4; 24.14.
4. *Common Worship*, p. 125.
5. This thanksgiving is taken from *Patterns for Worship*, Church House Publishing, 1995, pp. 137–8, and is based on 1 Corinthians 15.
6. This prayer is taken from *Patterns for Worship*, p. 185, and is based on Ephesians 3.20-21.

CHAPTER 5

1. Luke 3.3 – the same words are used for the preaching of the message and its content.
2. Luke 4.18.
3. For a thorough linking of each of the terms used here with themes in Acts, see L.T. Johnson, *The Gospel of Luke*, pp. 402–3.
4. Edwin Hatch; *Mission Praise*, no. 67.
5. John Cosin, based on *Veni, creator Spiritus*; *Mission Praise*, no. 90.
6. Charles Wesley; *Mission Praise*, no. 525.
7. A small number of Greek manuscripts omit the Greek words 'And they worshipped him'. For that reason the words do not appear in some English translations (including the New English Bible and the Revised Standard Version). Most scholars now regard the phrase as original to Luke's account.

Further Reading

All of the standard commentaries on Luke's Gospel have a section on Luke 24. In the shorter commentaries, this is not likely to go into very much detail on the passages discussed here. In preparing this study, I have drawn on a range of commentators but I would particularly commend for preachers:

Joel Green, *The Gospel of Luke*, The New International Commentary on the New Testament, Eerdmans, 1997.

Luke Timothy Johnson, *The Gospel of Luke*, Sacra Pagina, Liturgical Press, 1991.

John Nolland, *Luke 18.35–24.53*, Word Biblical Commentary 35c, Word, 1993.

The short study by Michael Wilcock, *The Message of Luke*, The Bible Speaks Today, IVP, 1979, is very well written and remains a useful source of ideas.

For those who want to explore the issue of the Emmaus road story and the interpretation of Scripture, I would also recommend:

R.W. L. Moberly, *The Bible, Theology and Faith: A Study of Abraham and Jesus*, Cambridge Studies in Christian Doctrine, Cambridge, 2000, especially chapter 2, 'Christ as the Key to Scripture: The Journey to Emmaus'.

Notes on the Order for Daily Prayer

Christians in every generation have found it helpful to pray and listen to Scripture using a prepared form, sometimes called a Daily Office. A very simple office is provided here for readers of this book who are not used to praying in this way and who want to set their Bible reading in the context of daily prayer.

It is helpful to find a regular time and place each day. Choose the time of day that is most convenient and helpful for you. There are six sections in each chapter and psalms are suggested for the six weekdays. The Preparation begins with a sentence of Scripture, an opening psalm and an opportunity for quiet prayer.

The Word of God suggests a psalm for each day. The psalms chosen are those used by many in the Church for the season of Easter. There is then space to read the set Bible passage and the notes.

The prayers are in response to the Word of God. Offer your own prayers of intercession in the place suggested. It may help to keep a short list of people and situations you pray for regularly.

Most of the material here is taken from Morning and Evening Prayer in *Common Worship*. If you find this way of praying helpful, you may want to explore a more developed form of the Daily Office. One example is *Celebrating Common Prayer*, Mowbray, 1992.

An Order for Daily Prayer

Preparation

Jesus said: 'I am the resurrection and the life. Those who believe in me, even though they die, will live, and everyone who lives and believes in me will never die. Do you believe this?' (John 11.25-26).

The Easter Anthems (or Psalm 95)

Christ our Passover has been sacrificed for us,
so let us celebrate the feast,
not with the old leaven of corruption and wickedness:
but with the unleavened bread of sincerity and truth.
Christ once raised from the dead dies no more:
death has no more dominion over him.
In dying he died to sin once, for all:
in living he lives to God.
See yourselves therefore as dead to sin:
and alive to God in Jesus Christ our Lord.
Christ has been raised from the dead:
the firstfruits of those who sleep.
For as by man came death:
by man has come also the resurrection of the dead;
For as in Adam all die:
even so in Christ shall all be made alive.

(From 1 Corinthians 5, Romans 6 and 1 Corinthians 15)

The night has passed and the day lies open before us;
Let us pray with one heart and mind.

Silence is kept.

As we rejoice in the gift of this new day,
so may the light of your presence, O God,
set our hearts on fire with love for you,
now and for ever.
Amen.

The Word of God

> Morning by morning he wakens –
> wakens my ear
> to listen as those who are taught (Isaiah 50.4).

A Psalm from the following table:

Monday	81
Tuesday	135
Wednesday	139
Thursday	33
Friday	30
Saturday	66

Bible reading (using the passage for the day)

Reflection on the Bible reading

Reading the notes

Prayers

The short prayer for the day (from the notes)

Intercessions are offered

The Lord's Prayer
Our Father in heaven,
hallowed be your name,
your kingdom come,
your will be done,
on earth as in heaven.

Give us today our daily bread.
Forgive us our sins
as we forgive those who sin against us.
Lead us not into temptation
but deliver us from evil.
For the kingdom, the power,
and the glory are yours,
now and for ever.
Amen.

Almighty God,
we thank you for the gift of your holy word.
May it be a lantern to our feet,
a light to our paths,
and a strength to our lives.
Take us and use us
to love and serve all people
in the power of the Holy Spirit
and in the name of your Son,
Jesus Christ, our Lord.
Amen.

If you have enjoyed using this Emmaus Bible Resource, you may be interested in *Emmaus – The Way of Faith*. This resource is designed to help churches welcome people into the Christian faith and the life of the Church.

Emmaus has three stages – contact, nurture and growth. It encourages the vision of the local church for evangelism and gives practical advice on how to develop contact with those outside the Church. The material includes a 15-week nurture course that covers the basics of the Christian life and four growth books that offer Christians an opportunity to deepen their understanding of Christian living and discipleship.

All the group notes are fully photocopiable.

The authors are Stephen Cottrell, Steven Croft, John Finney, Felicity Lawson and Robert Warren.

Visit our web site www.natsoc.org.uk/emmaus, email any enquiries to: emmaus@c-of-e.org.uk or call 020 7898 1524.

Introduction
Second edition
£4.95   0 7151 4963 6
Essential background to both the theology and practice of Emmaus and includes material on how to run the course in your own church.

Leading an Emmaus Group
£4.95   0 7151 4905 9
Straightforward and direct guide to leading both Nurture and Growth groups. It lays a biblical framework for group leadership.

Contact
£4.95   0 7151 4873 7
Explores ways that your church can be involved in evangelism and outreach.

Nurture
£17.50   0 7151 4874 5
A 15-session course covering the basics of Christian life and faith.

Growth: Knowing God
£17.50   0 7151 4875 3
Four short courses for growing Christians: Living the Gospel; Knowing the Father; Knowing Jesus; and Come, Holy Spirit.

Growth: Growing as a Christian
£17.50   0 7151 4876 1
Five short courses for growing Christians: Growing in Prayer; Growing in the Scriptures; Being Church; Growing in Worship; and Life, Death and Christian Hope.

Growth: Christian Lifestyle
£17.50   0 7151 4877 X
Four short courses for growing Christians: Living Images; Overcoming Evil; Personal Identity; and Called into Life.

Growth: Your Kingdom Come
£15.00   0 7151 4904 0
This Growth book looks in depth at two main issues, the Beatitudes and the Kingdom.

OTHER RELATED TITLES:

Praying Through Life
Stephen Cottrell
£7.95   0 7151 4902 4
Aimed at those starting out in the Christian faith and at all who find prayer difficult, or want to journey deeper in their faith.

Travelling Well – A Companion Guide to the Christian Faith
Stephen Cottrell and Steven Croft
£6.95   0 7151 4935 0
Provides instruction for important areas in Christian life such as prayer, reading the Bible, worship and relating faith to daily life. Ideal for adult Christians who are beginning the journey of faith.

In the same series:

Missionary Journeys, Missionary Church

Acts 13–20

Steven Croft

The book of Acts is the most exciting and dramatic book in the New Testament. Throughout Christian history, men and women have returned to the book of Acts to find their faith and ministry renewed and rekindled.

ISBN 0 7151 4972 5   Price £7.95

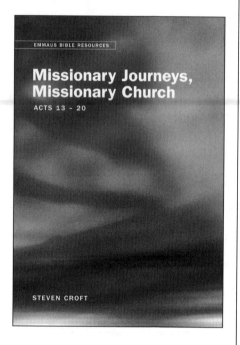

EMMAUS BIBLE RESOURCES

Missionary Journeys, Missionary Church

ACTS 13 - 20

STEVEN CROFT

This dramatic presentation of the earliest days of the Church calls a new generation to a journey of encounter, faith and witness.

Dr Bridget Nichols
Lay Chaplain to the Bishop of Ely

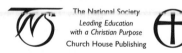

The National Society
*Leading Education
with a Christian Purpose*
Church House Publishing

**Church House Bookshop, 31 Great Smith Street, London, SW1P 3BN
Tel: 020 7898 1300, Fax: 020 7898 1305, www.chbookshop.co.uk**